LENINGRAD

Masha Nordbye

Photography by Patricia Lanza

WOR/947.4

SURREY COUNTY LIBRARY

GW00371127

ODYSSEY GUIDES
Hong Kong

91-670489

© The Guidebook Company Ltd 1991
All rights reserved.

Grateful acknowledgement is made to the following authors and publishers for permissions granted:

North Point Press for
The Noise of Time, translated by Clarence Brown, © Princeton University Press, 1965. Published by North Point Press and reprinted by permission.

Princeton University Press for
The Road to Bloody Sunday: The role of Father Gapon and the Assembly in the Petersburg Massacre of 1905 by Walter Sablinsky,
© Princeton University Press 1976.

Alfred A Knopf Inc for
The Road to Calvary by Alexei Tolstoy, translated by Edith Bone

Chatto & Windus and A P Watt Ltd. for
The Overcoat by Nikolai Gogol, translated by Constance Garnett

Random House Inc. and William Heinemann Ltd for
Among the Russians, © Colin Thubron, 1983

Distribution in the UK, Ireland and certain Commonwealth countries by
Hodder & Stoughton, Mill Road, Dunton Green, Sevenoaks, Kent, TN13 2YA

Editor: Deke Castleman
Series Editor: Rose Borton
Picture Editor: Caroline Robertson
Map Design: Bai Yiliang
Design: Aubrey Tse
Cover Concept: Raquel Jaramillo and Aubrey Tse
Excerpts: Andrew Coe
Photography by Patricia Lanza, with additional contributions from Masha Nordbye pages 19, 45, 85(bottom), 132 and 152.

ISBN: 962-217-176-1

British Library Cataloguing in Publication Data has been applied for.

Produced by Twin Age Ltd
Printed in Hong Kong

Cover: Samson fountain, Pedrodvorets

Contents

Introduction

by Andrew Coe

Between the slate grey skies and leaden waters of the Gulf of Finland (an arm of the Baltic Sea) lie the white columns and baroque decorations of Leningrad, one of the most beautiful cities in the world. It comes as a shock to see the ornate structures of Leningrad in these surroundings, only five hundred miles south of the Arctic Circle. This disorientation is at the heart of Leningrad's character, because the city has only a loose cultural connection with the flat pine forests—the typical Russian landscape—that spread out to the east. Where Leningrad really finds its soul is in the Neva River which winds around the 101 islands of the city. In those dark waters, Leningrad sees its own mirror-image: huge, pale and ornate structures rippling on the waves. Leningrad is a city passionately absorbed with itself, and this spirit of city-centrism has led to some of the great artistic achievements of Russian culture and also to some of the most violent political upheavals.

The Neva, which is only 67 kilometers long, is a broad and muddy river that flows west over a marshy plain from the enormous Lake Ladoga into the Gulf of Finland. At its mouth it widens into a delta made up of the 101 islands that comprise the present city of Leningrad. The Finnish border is only 175 kilometers away to the northeast, and Moscow is 540 kilometers in the opposite direction. Leningrad is on the same latitude as Anchorage, Alaska, and during the winter the sun shines blearily on the horizon for a few hours around noon. In June and July the sky is light 24 hours a day, nobody can sleep, and the city celebrates this astronomical bounty with its "White Nights" cultural festival.

As you walk along the embankments, one of the first things that strikes you is the light that washes over the city. Joseph Brodsky, the Nobel prize-winning poet who was born in Leningrad, said: "It's the northern light, pale and diffused, one in which memory and eye operate with unusual sharpness. In this light...a walker's thoughts travel farther than his destination..." The next thing you notice is the unusual unity of the buildings. In the heart of the city, none of the buildings are more than four or five stories and while they may have been built in different styles, they all embody an aspiration for grace and elegance. The spaces between the buildings have been designed in harmony as well: the river is lined with heavy brown granite embankments that provide a solid base for the airy structures that rise above them, and even the bridge railings are small masterpieces of ornate ironwork. The last thing that a pedestrian will remark is the sheer size of Leningrad's great buildings. The white pilasters of the Hermitage—one of the greatest museums in the world—seem to stretch for miles along the south embankment of the Neva. In the outskirts, the imperial retreats at Petrodvorets and Pushkin rival Versailles for grandeur.

These unique characteristics of Leningrad are the legacy of Peter the Great, who founded the city in 1703. He built the city on the swampy islands at the mouth of the Neva River first as a fortress to repel the Swedish army. When the Swedes were no longer a threat, the city, then called St Petersburg, became a window on the West. From this perch on the edge of the imperial domain, Russia could venture into Europe, learn of the great intellectual and technological advances being made, and begin to drag itself out of the Middle Ages. Momentoes to Peter the Great are scattered throughout the city. On the Petrogradskaya Storona sits his cabin, the first house in the city, a simple Dutch-style dwelling where he spent his summers, eschewing the trappings of royalty. The Kunstkammer in the Museum of Anthropology and Ethnography contains Peter the Great's collection of "monsters", freak animal and human embryos—a tribute to his restless curiosity and to his bloody-mindedness. Next to the Admiralty Building stands the enormous statue of Peter the Great known as the Bronze Horseman, a figure that has brought solace and madness to characters in Russian literature from Pushkin and Gogol to the present day. And, in the ultimate tribute to his memory, the residents of Leningrad call their city "Peter," and in doing so reject another leader whose name is also entwined with the city.

In the Soviet Union, Leningraders have a reputation for aloofness and arrogance and for being less than totally Russian. Ask a Muscovite about Leningrad, and he will say, "Forget about it; Moscow is Russia; Moscow is where it's happening." He is right: Moscow is Russia, in all its awfulness, giantism and claustrophobia, and all the latest cultural and political ideas are in the air. Leningraders do not mind, however. Their city is not exactly a backwater: it is a huge and bustling seaport and industrial center of 4,000,000 inhabitants. If Leningrad is not on the cutting edge, that's all right, because the city has enough cultural patrimony to last centuries. Every time somebody reads Gogol or Dostoevsky or sees a performance of *Boris Godunov*, *The Nutcracker* or *Swan Lake*, Leningrad's bounty flowers again. And Leningraders still have the graceful streets, the buildings scaled to human size and the reflection in the Neva.

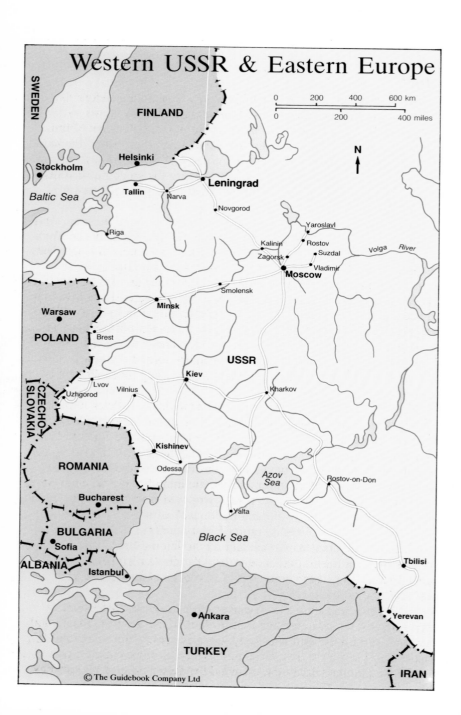

Western USSR & Eastern Europe

SWEDEN

FINLAND

0   200   400   600 km
0   200   400 miles

N

Helsinki

Stockholm

Leningrad

Baltic Sea   Tallin   Narva

Novgorod

Riga

Yaroslavl

Kalinin   Rostov

Zagorsk   Suzdal   Volga   River

Vladimir

Moscow

Smolensk

Minsk

Warsaw

POLAND   Brest

USSR

Kiev

Lvov   Vilnius   Kharkov

Uzhgorod

CZECHO-SLOVAKIA

Kishinev

ROMANIA   Odessa

Azov Sea   Rostov-on-Don

Bucharest   Yalta

BULGARIA   Black Sea

Sofia

ALBANIA   Istanbul

Tbilisi

Ankara   Yerevan

TURKEY

IRAN

© The Guidebook Company Ltd

History

The delta at the mouth of the Neva River was settled long before the founding of Leningrad, first called St Petersburg. The Neva was an important trading route between Northern Europe and Asia, and Finns, Swedes and Russians established settlements there at one time or another and frequently fought over the land. In the early 17th century, Russia's "Time of Troubles", the nation's military power was so debilitated that Midhail, the first of the Romanov czars, was forced to sign a treaty ceding the land to Sweden in 1617.

After Peter the Great returned from his tour of Holland, England and Germany, one of his first actions was to oust the Swedes from the Neva delta. In the winter of 1702-1703, Russian forces attacked and captured Swedish forts at Nyenshatz, a few miles upstream from the river's mouth, and Noteborg on Lake Ladoga. Peter ordered that the keys to the forts be nailed to their gates, and these two keys, hanging from a sailing ship, became the symbol of the future St Petersburg. On May 16, 1703, seven weeks after ousting the Swedes, Peter the Great lay the foundation stone of the Peter and Paul Fortress on an island near where the Neva divides into its two main branches. The primary role of the new settlement was as a military outpost, but right from the beginning Peter had greater designs.

While the construction of the fortress was underway, Peter lived in a rough log cabin nearby and from it planned his future capital. He decided that the hub of the new city was to be on the opposite bank of the Neva, at the present site of the Admiralty. Here he founded Russia's first great shipyard, where he built his navy. The construction of the city was to begin along the banks of the river and radiate inland along broad avenues from the shipyards. Peter's project was hampered from the start by the occasional flooding of the Neva and by the lack of workers willing to move to the cold and isolated swamp. With typical ruthlessness, he ordered the conscription of 40,000 laborers to lay the foundations and dig the canals. It is estimated that at least 10,000 people died from disease, exhaustion and floods during the first few years. "The town is built on bones", the saying goes.

In 1712, three years after the Swedes were finally and decisively defeated, Peter the Great decreed that St Petersburg was now the capital of the Russian Empire. Unfortunately, the aristocracy and merchants did not share his enthusiasm. Peter did not have the time or patience to persuade them, so he simply commanded the thousand leading families

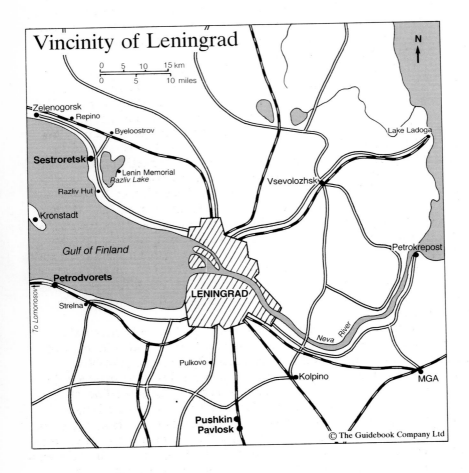

Vincinity of Leningrad

0 5 10 15 km
0 5 10 miles

Zelenogorsk
Repino
Byeloostrov
Sestroretsk
Lenin Memorial
Razliv Lake
Razliv Hut
Kronstadt
Lake Ladoga
Vsevolozhsk
Gulf of Finland
Petrokrepost
Petrodvorets
To Lomonosov
Strelna
LENINGRAD
Neva River
Pulkovo
Kolpino
MGA
Pushkin
Pavlosk

© The Guidebook Company Ltd

N

and five hundred most prominent merchants to build houses in the new capital. Aside from the Peter and Paul Fortress and Peter's cabin, the notable buildings of this era still standing are the Menshikov and Kikin Palaces, the Alexander Nevsky Monastery and the Monplaisir Palace at Petrodvorets. The construction of St Petersburg was the first time—but certainly not the last—that the hand of the State intervened on a national scale in the lives of the Russian masses.

By 1725, the year of Peter's death, St Petersburg had a population of 75,000 unwilling subjects. For the next few years, the future of the new capital was shaky due to the lack of a strong hand like Peter's. The council which ruled Russia under the twelve-year-old Peter II moved the imperial court back to Moscow and thousands of people thankfully left the half-built city. They stayed away until Peter II's early death, after which Empress Anna took the reins and in 1732 decreed that the capital would return to St Petersburg. Under Anna, the second great phase of the construction of St Petersburg began. She hired Bartolomeo Rastrelli, the son of an Italian sculptor hired by Peter the Great, to build her a Winter Palace (no longer standing), the first permanent imperial residence in the city. She also ordered the construction of an 80'-long 33'-high ice palace complete with rooms and ice furniture on the frozen Neva. This was built for a courtier who had been unfaithful to her and was forced to marry an ugly Kalmyk tribeswomen from Central Asia in a mock ceremony. They were stripped naked and had to spend the night in the ice palace with only each other for warmth.

Anna died the same winter, and after the brief rule of another child czar, Ivan VI, the Empress Elizabeth took the throne and built many of the most important buildings in Leningrad. By this time (1741-61), Rastrelli and other imported European architects had developed a style that later became known as Elizabethan rococo. Like a wedding cake, the basic structures disappeared underneath an ornate icing of pilasters, statuary and reliefs. The other recurrent theme was size. These buildings did not reach for the heavens like the churches of the Moscow Kremlin; they sprawled across acres of flat countryside. Huge architectural clusters like the Winter Palace and the Hermitage and the palaces at Peterhof and Pushkin, all painted an ethereal turquoise, were testament mostly to Elizabeth's power to do as she pleased. By the end of her rule, St Petersburg looked more like a stage set, with broad avenues built for parades and palaces like props for some grandiose drama, than a working city.

After Elizabeth's death, another weak csar, Peter III, took the throne and quickly died after forging an unpopular alliance with Prussia. The sceptre was handed to his wife, Catherine II, an independently-minded German princess who ruled the empire for 24 years. Under Catherine, later dubbed "the Great", St Petersburg solidified its position as the artisitic and political center of the empire, as intellectuals flocked to the now-thriving academies of Arts and Sciences. The latest political ideas from western Europe were hotly debated among the aristocracy, and the streets and squares of the city were dotted with sculptures crafted by the finest European artists, including the enormous "Bronze Horseman" portrait of Peter the Great cast by the Frenchman, Falconet. At the end of Catherine's reign in 1796, there was a profound sense of achievement in St Petersburg; in less than a century it had become one of the leading cities in the world. But there was also unease: the winds of change were blowing, and no one knew how to reconcile the new political ideas of St Petersburg with the profoundly conservative and deeply religious Russian countryside.

Catherine's son,

the mentally unstable Paul I, built a fortress variously known as the Mikhailovsky or Engineer's Palace to protect himself from conspirators against the throne. His paranoia proved justified, because in 1801, just twelve days after he moved in, his own courtiers strangled him to death. His successor was Alexander I, whose liberal reforms during the first half of his reign were wildly popular among the aristocracy and intelligentsia. The latter half of Alexander's rule was less successful, and a number of revolutionary cells were formed within the aristocracy to overthrow the imperial system. When Alexander died in December, 1825, these cells were violently opposed to the accession of his anointed successor, his younger brother Nicholas, who was known to be a conservative and sympathetic to the Prussians. A group of guards officers, later known as "Decembrists", took over the Senate Square and demanded a constitutional government. Nicholas ordered the army's cannons to fire on them, and the Decembrists fled in confusion. The main plotters were arrested and interned in the Peter and Paul Fortress, where five of them were executed and 115 were sent to Siberia. In 1849, this fortress was also the prison for the writer, Fyodor Dostoevsky, and the rest of the Petrashevsky Circle of socialist revolutionaries. Under Nicholas's orders, they were sentenced to death, led before a firing squad and then reprieved at the last minute and exiled to Siberia.

The period from Nicholas I through the Russian Revolution in 1917 was an era of more or less constant political repression of the aristocracy and intelligensia. Paradoxically, in St Petersburg it was the time of a great flowering of creativity that has given us some of the masterpieces of world literature, music and ballet, with writers like Pushkin, Gogol and Dostoevsky; the "Mighty Band" of the composers Rimsky-Korsakov, Mussorgsky and Brordin; and the choreographers of the Kirov Ballet, whose dances are still performed today.

Political turmoil proceeded apace with the artistic ferment during the latter half of the 19th century. St Petersburg was the center, of course, and a number of prominent revolutionary theorists, including the anarchist, Mikhail Bakunin, and the writer, Nikolai Chernyshevsky, spent time in the Peter and Paul Fortress. In March of 1881 these activities finally bore fruit when a terrorist cell called the People's Freedom Group succeeded in mortally wounding Czar Alexander II with a bomb on the banks of the Griboyedov Canal. The Church of the Resurrection, inspired by St Basil's in Moscow, was built on that spot by his son Alexander III to commemorate the assassination. This led to more decades of oppression under Alexander III and Nicholas II, which only served to heighten the political unrest. By this time the imperial system was not only unpopular among the St Petersburg elite but throughout Russian society.

Russia got a prelude of its future in 1905, when a series of strikes by soldiers and workers led to a huge demonstration in St Petersburg. A radical priest named Father Gapon led thousands of workers in a march to the Winter Palace to present a petition to Nicholas II. As they entered Palace Square, soldiers opened fire and hundreds of unarmed protestors were killed. "Bloody Sunday" shocked the nation and galvanized the revolutionary movement. Socialist intellectuals and workers formed mass parties for the first time and demanded a share of the power. Nicholas gave them a weak advisory body named the Duma, which was accepted by the moderates but not by the extreme left, and arrested as many revolutionary rabble-rousers as he could. Trotsky went to jail and Lenin escaped to Switzerland.

When Russia went to war against Germany in 1914, St Petersburg's name was changed to Petrograd to avoid the Germanic implications of having a "burg" at the end of its name. World War I was disasterous for the Russian empire. The long and bloody war in the trenches sapped the economically and politically weak nation. Back in St Petersburg, the Czar and the Duma fought for power, while the Charles Manson-like priest, Rasputin, played mind games with the Czarina and her circle, and the people starved. On March 12, 1917 the people of the capital rioted. They killed policemen, broke open the jail and set the courthouse on fire. The soldiers stationed in the city refused to quell the rioters; instead, they joined them. Two days later the Czar abdicated, and Russia was ruled by the Provisional Government led by the socialist leader, Alexander Kerensky.

In April, 1917 Vladimir Lenin arrived in Petrograd's Finland Station after a decade of exile and plotting and was met by a cheering mass of thousands. From the top of an armored car in front of the station Lenin gave a speech rallying his Bolshevik Party and their allies, the Soviets of Workers and Soldiers, against Kerensky's government. There followed months of agitation and attempted revolution which culminated in the night of November 7, 1917. The battleship, Aurora, under the control of the Bolsheviks, fired one shell at the Winter Palace, giving the signal for the Bolshevik troops to storm the palace and the other principal govern-ment buildings. The party of Lenin, Trotsky and Stalin was in command

of the Russian Empire. A month later Lenin ordered the formation of the Extraordinary Commission for the Suppression of Counterrevolution, the Cheka—later known as the KGB—and the Soviet state as we know it was born.

That was the easy part; the hard part was consolidating power. For the next three years, civil war raged through the nation. The Soviets were attacked by first the Germans, then the White Russian army and the British Royal Navy. During that time, Petrograd's population dropped from two and a half million to 720,000, due to hardship. In March of 1918, Lenin moved the Soviet government to Moscow, because Petrograd was vulnerable to a German attack - and perhaps also because of his distaste for the artificial imperial city.

On Lenin's death in 1924, Petrograd, which had been given the honorific "The Cradle of the Revolution", was renamed Leningrad, after a man who publicly despised the city and spent less than a year of his life there. Ominously, that same year there was a great flood in his namesake

An Opinionated Assessment

The Great Russians, of whom there are 52,000,000 in European Russia, migrated in early times from their original homes towards the E., driving the Finnish peoples before them. They have, however, to some extent mingled with the Finnish race, which probably accounts for the broad faces, flat noses, and other Mongolian features found frequently among them. They now occupy not only 'Great Russia' (i.e. N. and Central Russia, with the N.E. part of the Black Earth region), but also E. and S.E. Russia, the former territory of the Tartar Khans. Their speech, customs, and character are spread over the whole empire. Physically they are blond, blue-eyed, and vigorous, with broad shoulders and bull necks, often somewhat clumsy and with a strong tendency to obesity. Their character has been influenced not only by a long history of subjugation to feudal despotism, but also by the gloomy forests, the unresponsive soil, and the rigorous climate, and especially by the enforced inactivity of the long winters. In disposition they are melancholy and reserved, clinging obstinately to their traditions, and full of self-sacrificing devotion to Tzar, Church, and feudal superior. They are easily disciplined, and so make excellent soldiers, but have little power of independent thinking or of initiation. The normal Great Russian is thus the mainstay of political and economic inertia and reaction. Even the educated Russian gives comparatively little response to the actual demands of life; he is more or less the victim of fancy and temperament, which sometimes lead him to a despondent slackness, sometimes to emotional outbursts. Here we have the explanation of the want of organization, the disorder, and the waste of time which strike the western visitor to Russia. This pessimistic outlook finds expression in the word that is forever on Russian lips— 'it doesn't matter'; the Russian derives his faults as well as his virtues from his 'wide nature'. The important and fascinating literature of Russia reflects this dreamy and melancholy outlook on life, which is seen also in the national songs and music.

Karl Baedeker, Russia: A Handbook for Travelers, *1914*

city. During the next two decades Moscow became the center of the cultural and political life, while Leningrad became identified as a center of shipbuilding and industry; by 1939 it had more than 3,100,000 inhabitants. Its tradition of political assassination nevertheless continued with the 1934 shooting of Leningrad party leader, Sergei Kirov, at the Smolny Institute. Some say that Stalin was behind the shooting, and he certainly used it as the excuse to start the purges of 1934-36 in which thousands of Communist Party members were killed.

Leningrad received its next great blow during World War II. For 900 days from September, 1941 to January, 1944 the German Army laid siege to the city and hundreds of thousands of inhabitants died, adding more bones to the foundations. (See the Siege of Leningrad, p.70–71). Stalin instigated another purge in 1948-49, known as "The Leningrad Case", in which many of the city's top party members vanished forever or were sent to Siberia. In this purge it was apparent that the Moscow leadership remained suspicious of the Leningrad party hierarchy, because they retained some of the idealism of the original revolutionaries.

The years following the war were devoted to reconstruction of the center and the development of huge satellite suburbs to the south. Luckily, the government banned high-rises in the center of the city sustaining Catherine the Great's edict that no building shall be higher than the Winter Palace. The population now approaches four million, and the city is the second most important industrial centre after Moscow. Culturally, Leningrad has not scaled the same heights as it did in the 19th century, but its great ballet tradition at the Kirov and literary talents such as the dissident poets, Anna Akhmatova and Joseph Brodsky, keep hope alive.

It is interesting to speculate on what would have happened to the Soviet Union if Lenin had kept the capital in Petrograd. It is doubtful that the Soviet Government would have been able to keep as firm a grip on the lives of every inhabitant across the 6,000-mile-wide nation as it did in Moscow. Lenin's whole career was aimed at taking power and holding it, and the goals of socialist revolution were definitely secondary. If he had stayed on the Baltic—in a city Dostoevsky called "the most abstract and premeditated city on the whole round world"—it is possible that the northern light and the extravagant, un-Russian architecture would have tempered the cold and brutally realistic tempers of Lenin, Stalin and the other Soviet leaders, and they would have crafted a more fanciful and less totalitarian system.

Culture

A political and social history tells only half the story of Leningrad. Of equal consequence are the literary and artistic creations set in Leningrad, because in them writers and artists have created a parallel city that lives just as much in the minds of the inhabitants as today's crowded, slightly shabby metropolis. From the reign of Elizabeth on, the realms of fiction, poetry, symphony, opera and ballet have all collaborated to produce a Leningrad of the mind that is one of the great artisitic creations of mankind.

Literature

In the earliest years of St Petersburg, the fate of the city was too doubtful to allow the production of great works of art. Peter the Great emphasized the practical sciences, particularly engineering, and his image of the city as a glorified barracks left little room for the arts. St Petersburg's first great fight to Russian culture, Mikhail Lomonosov, arrived in the city in 1736 and went on to become the director of the Academy of Sciences. Lomonosov was a kind a Russian Benjamin Franklin—a chemist, physicist, geologist, educator, historian and poet. He also had studied in the West and was a friend of the French philosopher, Voltaire. Lomonosov devoted his life to bringing the ideas of the European Enlightenment to Russia and at the same time tried to advance Russia's cultural thought in distinctly Russian ways. Of all Lomonosov's achievements, his greatest in the cultural sphere was his Russian grammar, which codified and encouraged the use of the language of the common people in Russian literature.

If Lomonosov was the genius of the 18th century, then Alexander Pushkin was the soul of the 19th century. Pushkin was born into an aristocratic family descended on one side from a Negro slave who was a favorite in the court of Peter the Great. In his 20s he led a life of aristocratic dissoluteness in salons and bordellos of the imperial capital and began to write light romantic poetry. Many of his friends were politically active young officers associated with the Decembrist group, which Pushkin was never asked to join because they considered him too frivolous for their revolutionary mission. Nevertheless, he wrote some mildly seditious poems and was exiled to the Caucuses in 1820.

During his exile from St Petersburg he wrote some of his most famous works, including his epic *Boris Godunov*, the story of the pretender to the

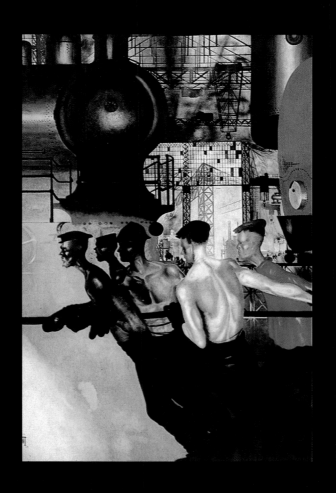

Russian throne at the start of the "Time of Troubles" in the early 17th century. At the end of his exile he began his masterpiece *Eugene Onegin*, a novel in verse about two star-crossed lovers, Onegin and Tatyana. Pushkin's last completed work was the apocalyptic poem "The Bronze Horseman", which is revered as the great work about St Petersburg. In it a young govenment clerk watches a huge storm cause a flood in St Petersburg which destroys most of the city and kills thousands, including his fiancée. Driven mad by grief, he comes upon Falconet's statue of Peter the Great, The Bronze Horseman, and he associates Peter's terrible imperial power with the destructive force of the flood. The mad clerk shakes his fist at the statue, and the horseman comes to life in a rage and chases him out of the square with a great clattering of bronze hoofs. In 1836 Pushkin was mortally wounded in a pistol duel over his wife's honor and died in January, 1837 at the age of 36. Immediately upon his death he was lionized as the greatest Russian writer, and that acclaim continues to this day.

Pushkin's mantle was inherited by Nikolai Gogol, a Ukranian-born writer, whose work is difficult to classify. At times, as in his play *The Inspector General*, he satirized the vast bureaucratic state that had taken over the Russian Empire. His famous short story "The Greatcoat" is more enigmatic. A petty government clerk in St Petersburg invests all his savings in a new overcoat, but as he is returning home late at night he loses it to a band of robbers. After he discovers that none of his superiors will help him find his coat he dies of grief, only to reappear on the streets of St Petersburg as an avenging ghost. Gogol followed "The Greatcoat" with "Dead Souls", which was to be the first volume of a projected trilogy envisioned as a sort of Russian "Divine Comedy" about sin, atonement and salvation. As he wrote the second volume, he began to go mad, thinking that the flames of hell were licking at his heels, and eventually threw the pages into the fire. He died in 1852 after doctors applied leeches and bled him to death.

The next great St Petersburg writer was Fyodor Dostoevsky, who, although anguished and epileptic, managed to live to a full lifespan. Dostoevsky studied to be a military engineer and fell in with the Petrashevsky Circle of socialist revolutionaries in St Petersburg. After being condemned to death and reprieved at the last minute, Dostoevksy was exiled to Omsk, Siberia, for four years. When he returned, he wrote *Memories from the House of the Dead* about his Siberian experiences and the acclaim at its publication in 1860 launched his career as a writer.

Most of Dostoevsky's novels were written in serial form for magazines, so he could stay one step ahead of his many creditors. He took his subject matter from popular melodramas and sensational newspaper stories and wrote about them with the methods of psychological realism, a form that he pioneered. His greatest novel, *Crime and Punishment* tells the story of Raskolnikov, an impoverished former student, who murders his landlady and feels such guilt that by the time he is finally brought to justice he welcomes it.

Late in life Dostoevsky became a devout believer in Orthodox Christianity. Luckily for world literature, he never lost his commitment to artistic realism, so his novels show the passionate struggle of trying to reach an ideal goal but never attaining it. When Dostoevsky died in 1881, thousands of Russians, ordinary citizens and fellow writers alike, accompanied his coffin to the Alexander Nevsky Monastery for a hero's burial.

After the Revolution, the center of literary activity moved to Moscow, although Leningrad has continued to produce great writers. In partial reaction to the Soviet State, many of these, like the poet Anna Akhmatova, have produced intensely personal visions rather than huge, all-encompassing epics.

Ballet

Russia made ballet a great art. Before the 19th century, ballet was little more than a music-hall phenomenon and distinctly inferior to opera. Russia's ballet tradition started in 1738 when the Empress Anna granted Jean-Baptist Lande, a French dance instructor, permission to open a dance school for children of the aristocracy. The Imperial Ballet School grew in importance but did not produce any significant innovations until Charles Didelot took over in 1801. Didelot was another French emigré, and he reorganized the school following the French classical model. The Imperial Ballet had the advantage of royal patronage and this prestige gave Didelot the impetus to raise the form to a higher level. He introduced elaborate narrative ballets with complicated sets that turned the performances into great theatrical experiences. The new Russian ballets, and the ballerinas, provided inspiration for a whole generation of writers, particularly Pushkin.

The next great era of Russian ballet began in 1847 when Marius Petipa joined the Imperial Ballet. In 1869 he became ballet master and choreographer and for the next 34 years he was the guiding light of Russian ballet. He choreographed over 60 ballets, many of them with

Russian themes, and worked with many Russian composers in producing distinctly Russian works of art. His most popular creations include *The Sleeping Beauty*, *The Nutcracker* and *Swan Lake*, all with music by Tchaikovsky. As news of his work spread throughout the dance world, Russian ballet became known for these exciting, large scale spectacles. His dancers also became world-famous and the standard for excellence: Anna Pavlova, Mikhail Fokine (who went on to become a choreographer) and Vaslav Nijinsky.

The Imperial Ballet lost some of its brightest stars when many dancers emigrated with Serge Diaghilev and his Ballets Russes company. Since the 1918 Revolution, the Moscow Ballet, with its flamboyant and emotional productions, has been considered the top Soviet company. However, the Kirov (the Soviet name for the Imperial company) continues to follow a more elegant and classical tradition and produce stars, and emigrés, like Rudolph Nureyev, Natalia Makarova and Mikhail Baryshnikov.

Music

The development of Russian music in St Petersburg followed the same patterns as literature, only later. In the 1830s and 40s, Mikhail Glinka, a close friend of Pushkin, composed many symphonies and two operas based on Russian folk songs from his childhood. Glinka put these folk themes together with many of Pushkin's poems and produced some of the first distinctly Russian musical works. One of his most famous pieces is *Rusland and Ludmilla*, an opera based on Pushkin's mock-romantic epic about the court of Kievan Russia.

By the mid-19th century, St Petersburg had become a major musical center and Berlioz, Verdi, Strauss and Wagner conducted their work there. In response to this invasion of Western talent, particularly Wagner, whom they believed had imperial aspirations, a group of Russian composers banded together to promote their own "Russian" music. Known as the "Mighty Band", they included Nikolai Rimsky-Korsakov, Alexander Borodin and Modest Mussorgsky. The "Band" followed Glinka's example and composed music based on folk songs and themes from Russian literature. Borodin's most famous work was the opera *Prince Igor*, which was based on old Russian heroic song and included the famous Eastern dance number, the Polovetsian Dances. Rimsky-Korsakov also wrote a number of operas based on mythic-historical themes from early Russian history and folklore. Mussorgsky, an epileptic like Dostoevsky, was the

A Cultural Extravaganza

*I*n the season of 1903-4 Petersburg witnessed concerts in the grand manner. I am speaking of the strange, never-to-be-surpassed madness of the concerts of Hofmann and Kubelik in the Nobility Hall during Lent. I can recall no other musical experiences, not even the premiere of Scriabin's Prometheus, that might be compared with these Lenten orgies in the white-columned hall. The concerts would reach a kind of rage, a fury. This was no musical dilettantism: there was something threatening and even dangerous that rose up out of enormous depths, a kind of craving for movement; a mute prehistorical malaise was exuded by the peculiar, the almost flagellant zeal of the halberdiers in Mikhaylovsky Square, and it whetted the Petersburg of that day like a knife. In the dim light of the gas lamps the many entrances of the Nobility Hall were beset by a veritable siege. Gendarmes on prancing horses, lending to the atmosphere of the square the mood of a civil disturbance, made clicking noises with their tongues and shouted as they closed ranks to guard the main entry. The sprung carriages with dim lanterns slipped into the glistening circle and arranged themselves in an impressive black gypsy camp. The cabbies dared not deliver their fares right to the door; one paid them while approaching, and then they made off rapidly to escape the wrath of the police. Through the triple chains the Petersburger made his way like a feverish little trout to the marble ice-hole of the vestibule, whence he disappeared into the luminous frosty building, draped with silk and velvet. The orchestra seats and the places behind them were filled in the customary order, but the spacious balconies to which the side entrances gave access were filled in bunches, like baskets, with clusters of humanity. The Nobility Hall inside is wide, stocky, and almost square. The stage itself takes up very nearly half the area. The gallery swelters in a July heat. The air is filled with a ceaseless humming like that of cicadas over the steppe.

Osip Mandelstam, The Noise of Time

most artistically ambitious of the "Band". He began by writing works based on Gogol's stories, which he considered were the closest to the Russian soul. Another piece tried to reproduce musically the babble in the marketplace at Nizhny Novgorod. Mussorgsky's two greatest works are the operas *Boris Godunov*, based on Pushkin's poem, and *Khovanshchina*, the first part of yet another unfinished trilogy. *Khovanshchina* is a kind of tone poem rendition of Russian-style chaos and social anarchy set at the end of the Time of Troubles just before Peter took the throne. While Mussorgsky was finishing this piece, he went mad and died a few weeks after Dostoevsky in 1881. He was buried by the writer's side in the Alexander Nevsky Monastery.

As in the other arts, music during the post-Revolution period, particularly after 1928, was marked by a decline in quality, not just in Leningrad but in all of the Soviet Union. Leningrad's greatest musical genius of the 20th century was Shostakovich, who produced works like *The Symphony of Socialism* described here:

It begins with the Largo of the masses working underground, an accelerando corresponding to the subway system; the Allegro, in its turn, symbolizes the gigantic factory machinery and its victory over nature. The Adagio represents the synthesis of Soviet culture, science and art. The Scherzo reflects the athletic life of the happy inhabitants of the Union. As for the Finale, it is the image of the gratitude and enthusiasm of the masses.

The abstraction has finally swallowed the people whole, and not a trace of humanity remains.

It is too early to tell if the current perestroika will lead to a new flowering of culture in Leningrad and, if it does, what arts will flourish. Times are so hard economically that people may not have time to step back and look at themselves. However, at least they have the room to create.

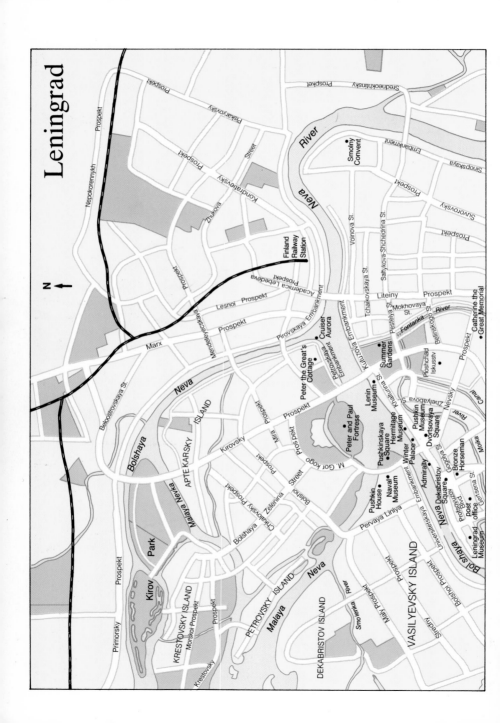

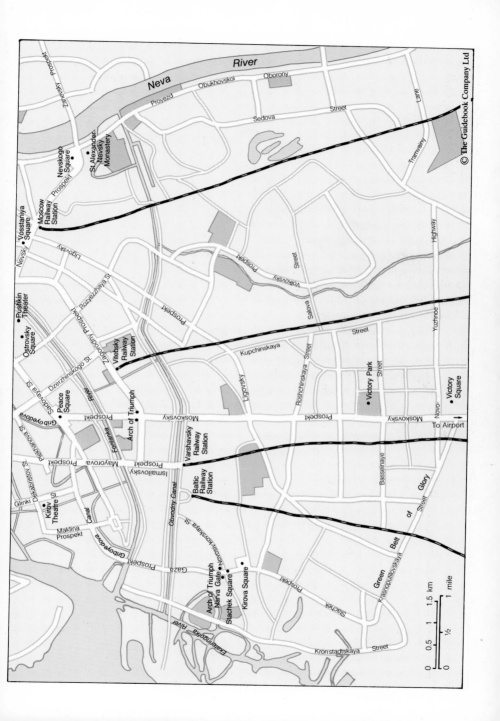

Getting Around

Orientation

Before sightseeing, look at a map and familiarize yourself with Leningrad. Once you know the general layout of the city, it is not difficult to find your way around by walking, or taking the bus, boat or Metro. Leningrad is 400 miles (640 km) north of Moscow on the same longitude as Helsinki, Finland and Anchorage, Alaska. The city is separated by the **Neva River**, which begins at Lake Ladoga and empties 46 miles (74 kilometres) later into the Gulf of Finland. At the tip of Vasilevsky Island, it splits into the Bolshaya (Big) and the Malaya (Little) Neva. The right bank of the Neva is known as the Petrogradskaya side (originally known as Birch Island), which includes the Zayachy, Petrogradsky, Aptekarsky and Petrovsky islands. The Kirovsky Islands lie farther to the north. Many of the main points of interest are found on the left bank of the Neva.

Leningrad was originally spread out over 101 islands; today, because of redevelopment, there are 44 islands, connected by 620 bridges linking over 100 waterways and canals that make up one-sixth of the area of the city. Leningrad is a treasure house of activity with over 50 museums, 20 theaters and concert halls, 60 stadiums and 2,500 libraries. The whole area, a museum of architecture, has some 200 palaces and historical landmarks. As a main port,over 5,000 ships dock here annually. Residents are proud of Leningrad; each parent gets a medallion for their newborn baby with the inscribed words, "Born in Leningrad".

Leningrad Metro

Like the Moscow Metro, the Metro in Leningrad is a fast and economical way to travel throughout the city, costing only five kopeks. Over 45 stations link the many sights and islands of Leningrad. The history of the Metro dates all the way back to Czar Alexander I. An engineer wanted to dig a tunnel from the city center to Vasilyevsky Island. The czar responded by ordering him not to "engage in any further hare-brained schemes in the future". On November 15, 1955, the first line of the Metro was opened.

Boat Tours

A number of boat tours run through Leningrad. If your tour does not include any, you can easily go on your own. Opposite the Hermitage

Museum are two docks on the Neva. The first is for a boat ride along the
Neva (another dock for a cruise on the Neva is opposite Decembrists'
Square). Here you can buy tickets—the times are posted on the kiosk. It
is a lovely cruise from the Hermitage to the Smolny Convent on a dou-
ble-decker boat that lasts about an hour. The second dock is for hydrofoils, the *Rockets*, to Peter's Summer Palace, Petrodvorets. The ride lasts
about 25 minutes and takes you past the city out into the Gulf of Finland.
(See also Petrodvorets in Vicinity of Leningrad section.)

A third boat trip takes you on a tour of the Leningrad canals. This
leaves from the Anichkov Bridge off Nevsky Prospekt and cruises along
the Fontanka and Moika rivers and Kryukov Canal, and lasts about 75
minutes.

Boats depart daily about every 15 minutes from May to September.
Commentaries are usually in Russian only. Tickets (in rubles) are inex-
pensive; but often, during nice weather, they sell out quickly. It is ad-
vised to buy tickets ahead of the time you wish to leave. Refreshments
are sold onboard each cruise for rubles.

Peter the Great

Peter the Great, one of Russia's most enlightened and driven rulers, pulled his country out of her dark feudal past into a status equal with her European neighbors. Possessing an intense curiosity toward foreign lands, he opened Russia's window to the West and became the first ruler to journey extensively outside Russia. Standing at six feet seven inches, with a passionate will and temper to match his great size, Peter I, against all odds, also built a city that became one of the most magnificent capitals in all of Europe.

Peter's father, Czar Alexei, ruled the Empire from 1645 to 1676. Alexei's first wife had 13 children; but only two, Fyodor and Ivan, were destined to inherit the throne. Natalya Naryshkin became Alexei's second wife and gave birth to a son named Peter in 1672.

When Alexei died, his son, Fyodor III, succeeded to the throne and reigned from 1676 to 1682. During this time, his half-brother, Peter, along with ill-favored Natalya, were sent away from Moscow to live in the country. Instead of the usual staunch upbringing within the Kremlin walls, Peter had the freedom to roam the countryside and make friends with peasant children. When Fyodor died, a rivalry broke out between the two families as to which son would gain the throne. Peter won the first battle and was proclaimed czar at the age of ten. But soon Ivan's side of the family spread rumors to the Streltsy, or Musketeers (the military protectors of Moscow), that the Naryshkins were plotting to kill Ivan. The Streltsy demanded that Peter's half-brother be crowned, too. So, for a time, the throne of Moscovy was shared by the two boys, the feeble-minded Ivan V and the robust Peter I. In actuality, however, it was Sophia, Peter's older half-sister, who ruled as Regent for seven years with the help of her lover, Prince Golitzin.

Peter spent most of this time back in the country, mainly engaged in studies that had a practical use. One fateful day, the young boy discovered a wrecked English boat that could sail against the wind. He had the boat repaired and learned how to maneuver it. Infatuated now with sailing, he also immersed himself in the study of mathematics and navigation. In addition, the young czar worked well with his hands and became an accomplished carpenter, blacksmith and printer; he even mended his own clothes. As a child, he loved to play soldiers, and drilled his companions in military maneuvers, eventually staging mock battles with weapons and in uniforms supplied by the royal arsenal. Peter was also fascinated with the techniques of torture. Later in his reign, fearing an assassination attempt, he would torture his first son, Alexei, to death.

Sophia was eventually removed from court affairs and sent off to live in Novodevichy Convent outside Moscow. When Ivan died, Peter I, at the age of 22, assumed the throne as the sole czar and took up his imperial duties with earnest. On the throne, his first real battle was against the Turks. His plan was to take the Sea of Azov at the mouth of the Don in order to gain access to the Black Sea. Peter built a fleet of ships, and for the first time in her history, Russia led a surprise attack from the water. The Turks were defeated and Russia had her first southern outlet to the sea.

After this successful campaign, Peter set off on a long journey to the West. He traveled to England, France, and Germany, and worked as a shipbuilder in Holland. Back home, the Streltsy, with the help of Sophia, began to organize a secret revolt to overthrow the Czar. Peter caught wind of their plans; upon his return, he captured and tortured almost 2,000 men and dissolved the corps. By this time, the now cultured ruler had lost interest in his first wife and sent her off to a convent in Zagorsk, the equivalent of divorce.

Peter was greatly impressed by Western ways and, to him, change symbolized Russia's path to modernizaton. Knee-length coats became the new fashion. One of the new state laws prohibited the growing of beards. Since the church taught that man was created in God's image (ie with a beard), many believed Peter I to be the Antichrist.

But Peter was as determined as ever to pull Russia out of her isolation. He tolerated new religions, allowing the practices of Catholics, Lutherans and Protestants, and even approving of the sacreligious scientific stance taken by Galileo. He exercised state control over the Russian Orthodox Church by establishing the Holy Synod. This supremacy of the Czar over the Russian Church lasted from 1721 until 1917. In 1721, Peter also declared himself Emperor of All Russia.

During the Great Northern Wars, while chasing the Swedes out of the Baltic area, Peter the Great began building the first Russian Navy on the Gulf of Finland. It was during this time that he met and fell in love with a good-natured peasant girl named Catherine, whom he later married; Empress Catherine ruled for two years after his death.

In 1703, Peter began the fanatic building of a new city in the north at a point where the Neva River drained into Lake Ladoga. The city was constructed on a myriad of islands, canals and swamps. The conditions were brutal and nearly 100,000 perished the first year alone. But within a decade, St Petersburg was a city of 35,000 stone buildings and the capital of the Russian Empire. Peter commissioned many well-known foreign architects: the Italian Rastrelli, the German Schlüter, the Swiss Trezzini and the Frenchman Leblond, who created Peter's Summer Palace of Petrodvorets. Montferrand later designed St Isaac's Cathedral, which took over 100 kilos of gold and 40 years to build. Peter brought the majesty of the West to his own doorstep. It was no small wonder that St Petersburg was nicknamed the Venice of the North.

Peter died looking out from his "window to the West". Today in Leningrad stands a monument to the city's founder, a statue of Peter the Great as the Bronze Horseman. The statue, made by the French sculptor, Falconet, shows Peter rearing up on a horse that symbolizes Russia, while trampling a serpent that opposes his reforms. Pushkin wrote that Peter "With iron bridle reared up Russia to her fate". By a great and forceful will, Peter the Great had successfully led Russia out of her darkness into the light of a Golden Age.

Sights

Peter and Paul Fortress

The origins of the city are traced to the Peter and Paul Fortress, Petropavlovskaya Krepost. Peter the Great was attracted to Zayachy Ostrov (Hare Island), situated between the right bank of the Neva and the Kronverk Strait, because of its small size and strategic position in the area. On May 16, 1703, the first foundation stone of the fortress, named after the apostles Peter and Paul, was laid by Peter himself. The fortress was designed to protect the city from the invading Swedes, and was built as an elongated hexagon with six bastions that traced the contours of the island. Over 20,000 workers were commissioned and, within only six months, the earthern ramparts were set in place. Work continued on the fortress, replacing the wooden buildings with brick and stone until its completion in 1725. The new walls were over 36 feet (12 meters) thick and 300 guns were installed. Soon after its completion, the fortress lost its military significance, and over the next 200 years it served instead as a political prison. In 1922, the fortress was opened as a museum. It is open from 11 am–6 pm (11 am–5 pm on Tuesdays), closed on Wednesdays.

Ironically, the first prisoner was Peter's son, Alexei, suspected of plotting against the czar. Peter supervised his son's torture and Alexei died here in 1718. (Alexei was buried by Peter beneath the staircase of the cathedral, so he would always be "trampled".) The history of the fortress is also closely connected with revolutionary movements. Catherine the Great locked up Alexander Radishchev, who criticized the autocracy and feudal system in his book *Voyages from St Petersburg to Moscow*. Later, in 1825, the Decembrists were placed in the Alexeyevsky Bastion, a special block for important prisoners. Five were executed on July 13, 1826, and hundreds of others were sentenced to hard labor in Siberia. Members of the Petrashevsky political movement, including Dostoevsky, were sent here in 1849, and sentenced to death. Only at the last minute did Nicholas I revoke the sentence. Nikolai Chernyshevsky wrote his influential novel, *What is To Be Done?*, while imprisoned here for two years in 1862. In the 1880s, many members of the Narodnaya Volya (Peoples Freedom Group) were placed in solitary-confinement cells in the Trubetskoi Bastion. In 1887, five prisoners were executed for the attempt on the life of Alexander III, including Lenin's brother, Alexander Ulyanov. The writer, Maxim Gorky, was incarcerated for

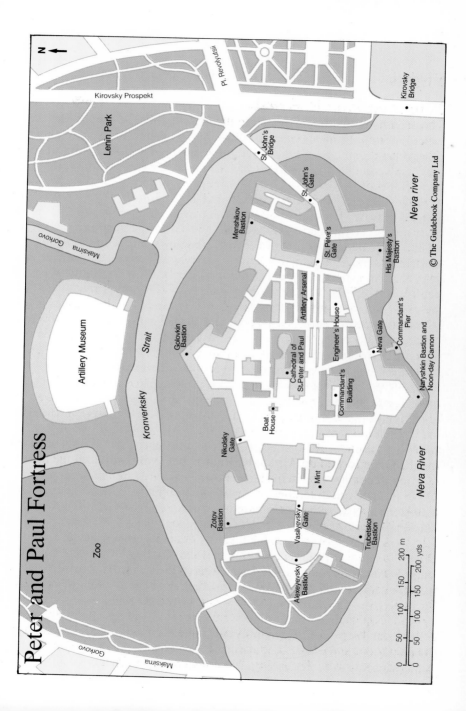

Peter and Paul Fortress

Zoo

Artillery Museum

Gorkovo

Maksima

Lenin Park

Kirovsky Prospekt

Pl. Revolyutsii

Kronverksky

Strait

Gorkovo

Maksima

Golovkin Bastion

Nikolsky Gate

Zotov Bastion

Alexeyevsky Bastion

Vasilyevsky Gate

Mint

Boat House

Cathedral of St.Peter and Paul

Commandant's Building

Trubetskoi Bastion

Menshikov Bastion

Artillery Arsenal

Engineer's House

St.John's Bridge

St.John's Gate

St.Peter's Gate

His Majesty's Bastion

Neva Gate

Commandant's Pier

Naryshkin Bastion and Noon-day Cannon

Neva river

Neva River

Kirovsky Bridge

© The Guidebook Company Ltd

| 0 | 50 | 100 | 150 | 200 m |

| 0 | 50 | 100 | 150 | 200 yds |

writing revolutionary leaflets. During the October 1917 Revolution, when the fortress's last stronghold was captured by the Bolsheviks and the political prisoners set free, a red lantern was hung in the Naryshkin Bastion, signaling the battleship *Aurora* to fire the first shot of the Revolution. Everyday a blank cannon shot is fired from the Naryshkin Bastion at noon. This tradition actually began in the 18th century to let the townspeople know the time. The nearest Metro stop to the fortress is Gorkovskaya.

The visitor's entrance to the fortress is at **St John's Gate**, on the east side of the island not far from Kirov Prospekt. After crossing St John's Bridge, you come to **St Peter's Gate** (1718), the main entrance and oldest unchanged structure of the fort. Hanging over the archway is a double-headed eagle, the emblem of the Russian Empire, along with bas-reliefs of the Apostle Peter. The carver, Konrad Osner, gave the Apostle the features of the czar. Beyond the gate is His Majesty's Bastion, used as a dungeon for Peter's prisoners.

A straight path leads to **St Peter and Paul Cathedral**, built between 1712 and 1732 in the Dutch style by the architect, Trezzini. Peter the Great laid the cornerstone. The cathedral, with its long slender golden spire topped with an angel holding a cross, is the focal point of the square. The belfry used to be the tallest structure in the whole country. (Today the TV tower is the tallest structure in Leningrad.) The tower clock plays the "Internationale" national anthem four times a day and the clock chimes every quarter hour.

Inside, the gilded wooden iconostasis was carved in 1722-26 and holds 43 icons. The cathedral is the burial place for over 30 czars and princes, including every czar from Peter I to Alexander III (except for Peter II). The sarcophagi of Alexander II and his wife took 17 years to carve from Altai jasper and Ural red quartz. Peter the Great himself chose his resting place to the right of the altar.

Outside again, with your back facing the cathedral entrance, on the right is a small pavilion with a statue of the Goddess of Navigation. The **Boat House** was built by Peter the Great in 1761 to store a small boat that he sailed as a child. Today, this "Grandfather of the Russian Fleet" is on display at the Central Naval Museum at 4 Pushkin Square on Vasilyevsky Island.

Directly in front of the cathedral is the yellow-white building of the **Mint** (1800–1806). In 1724, Peter the Great transferred the Royal Mint from Moscow to St Petersburg. The first lever press in the world was used here in 1811. The Mint still produces special coins, medals and badges. Beyond the Mint are the Alexeyevsky, Zotov and Trubetskoi Bastions, where many of the revolutionaries were imprisoned. The latter houses an exhibit which traces the history of prisoners who stayed in the cells.

As you leave the Cathedral, on the left side is the stone Commandant's Building, built as the commander's headquarters and the interrogation center for prisoners. It now houses the **Museum of History of St Petersburg and Petrograd from 1703 to 1917.** Next door, the old Engineer's House is now the **Architectural Museum of St Petersburg**, displaying many original drawings and drafts of the city. Both are closed on Wednesday. Behind these stands the **Neva Gate**, once known as the "Gate of Death", because prisoners were led through it to the execution spot. Now it leads to the beach area (with a spectacular view of the city) that is quite crowded in summer with sunbathers. The Walrus Club gathers here in winter to swim between the ice floes in the Neva!

Across The Kronverk Strait

Exiting the fortress by way of St John's Bridge takes you back to Kirov Prospekt. To the right is the **Kirov Bridge**, with a splendid view of the fortress. A short walk down Kirov Prospekt, to the left, leads to Metro stop, Gorkovskaya. The small path to the left of St John's Bridge circles around the Kronverk Strait. This path leads to a monument: a small obelisk, to the Decembrist revolutionaries, stands on the spot where Nicholas I executed the five leaders of the 1825 uprising. A witness account described the execution: "The hangmen made them stand on a bench and put white canvas hoods over their heads. Then the bench was knocked from under their feet. Three men whose ropes had broken fell on the rough boards of the scaffold bruising themselves. One broke his leg. According to custom, in such circumstances, the execution had to be canceled. But in an hour, new ropes were brought and the execution carried through".

Past the obelisk, on the right, is a large building that was once the artillery arsenal. Today it is the **Kronverk Artillery, Engineers and Signals Museum**, first formed by Peter the Great to display the history of Russian weaponry. It is open 11 am–6 pm, (closed on Mondays and Tuesdays).

Behind the museum is Lenin Park, stretching from the Strait to Maxim Gorky Prospekt, where the writer lived at no. 23 from 1914 to 1921. Inside the park is the Zoo, with over 1,000 animals, and the Planetarium. By the planetarium are the Lenin Komsomol Theater and the 3-D and first wide-screen Velikan (Vulcan) cinema, opened in 1956, seating 2,000.

Sergei Kirov (1886-1934), regional head of the Leningrad Party before he was murdered, lived at 26 Kirov Prospekt, not far from Leo Tolstoy Square. The house is now a museum, open 11 am–7 pm, Thursdays 2 pm-7 pm, Sundays 10 am–5pm. At 10 Kirov is Lenfilm Studios, founded in 1918.

Crossing Kirov Prospekt and walking east along the Neva (in the opposite direction to the fortress), you come to Revolution Square, formerly Trinity Square, where many of the first buildings of the city once stood. These included the Senate, Custom House and Troitsky Cathedral, where Peter was crowned Emperor in 1721. Today the square is a large garden. The **Museum of the October Revolution**, located at the northern end of the square at no. 14 Kuibishev, is in a mansion (1902) that formerly belonged to the ballerina, Matilda Kshesinskaya, the mistress of Nicholas II before he married. It is open 10 am–6 pm daily, (closed on Thursdays).

Continuing along Petrovskaya Embankment, you pass the two-ton granite figures of Shih-Tze, brought from Manchuria in 1907, poised on the steps by the Neva. In China, these sculptures, a cross between a lion and a frog, guarded the entrances to palaces. Behind them is the **Cottage of Peter the Great**, one of the oldest surviving buildings of the city. It was constructed in a mere three days in May 1703, out of pine logs painted to look like bricks. One room was a study and reception area and the other was used as a dining-room and bedroom. The largest door was five foot nine inches high—Peter stood at six foot seven! From here Peter directed the building of his fortress—with no stoves or chimneys, since Peter lived in the cottage only in summer. Once his summer palace was completed, Peter stopped living here altogether. In 1784, Catherine the Great encased the tiny house in stone to protect it. The cottage is now a museum, displaying his furniture, utensils and small boat, which Peter supposedly built and used to rescue fisherman on Lake Ladoga in 1690. A bronze bust of Peter is in the garden. The cottage is open 10 am–6 pm daily (closed on Tuesdays) and from November 11–April 30.

The Petition Of January 9, 1905

Most Humble and Loyal Address of the Workers of St. Petersburg Intended for Presentation to HIS MAJESTY on Sunday at two o'clock on the Winter Palace Square

SIRE:

We, the workers and inhabitants *of St. Petersburg, of* various estates, *our wives, our children, and our aged, helpless parents, come to Thee, O SIRE, to seek justice and protection. We are impoverished; we are oppressed, overburdened with excessive toil, contemptuously treated. We are not even recognized as human beings, but are treated like slaves who must suffer their bitter fate in silence and without complaint. And we have suffered, but even so we are being further pushed into the slough of poverty, arbitrariness, and ignorance. We are suffocating in despotism and lawlessness. O SIRE, we have no strength left, and our endurance is at an end. We have reached that frightful moment when death is better than the prolongation of our unbearable sufferings.*

Hence, we stopped work and told our employers that we will not resume work until our demands are fulfilled. We did not ask much; we sought only that without which there is no life for us but hard labor and eternal suffering. Our first request was that our employers agree to discuss our needs with us. But even this we were refused. We were prohibited even from speaking of our needs, since no such right is given us by law. The following requests were also deemed to be outside of the law: the reduction of the workday to eight hours; our mutual participation in determining the rates for our work and in the settlement of grievances that might arise between us and the lower managerial staff; to raise the minimum daily wages for unskilled workers, and for women as well, to one ruble; to abolish overtime work; to give our sick better medical attention without insults; and to arrange our workshops so that we might work there without encountering death from murderous drafts, rain, and snow.

According to our employers and managers, *our demands turned out to be illegal, our every request a crime, and our desire to improve our conditions an insolence, insulting* to them. *O SIRE, there are more than 300,000 of us but we are human beings in appearance only, for we,* with the rest of the Russian people, *do not possess a single human right, not even the right to speak, think, gather, discuss our needs, and take steps to improve our conditions.* We are enslaved, enslaved under the patronage and with the aid of Thy officials. *Anyone of us who dares to raise his voice in defense of the working class* and the people *is thrown into jail or exiled. Kindheartedness is punished as a crime. To feel sorry for a worker as a downtrodden, maltreated human being bereft of his rights is to commit a heinous crime!* The workers and the peasants are delivered into the hands of the bureaucratic administration, comprised of embezzlers of public funds and robbers, who not only care nothing for the needs of the people, but flagrantly abuse them. The bureaucratic administration brought the country to the brink of ruin, involved her in a humiliating war, and is leading Russia closer and closer to disaster. We, the workers and people, have no voice whatsoever in the spending of huge sums collected from us in taxes. We do not even know how the money, collected from the impoverished people, is spent. The people are deprived of the opportunity to express their wishes and demands, to participate in the establishment of taxes and public spending. The workers are deprived of the opportunity to organize into unions in order to defend their interests.

*O SIRE, is this in accordance with God's laws, by the grace of which Thou reignest? Is it possible to live under such laws? Would it not be preferable for all of us, the toiling people of Russia, to die? Let the capitalists-*exploiters of the working class *and officials, the embezzlers and plunderers of the Russian people, live and enjoy their lives.*

Translated by Walter Sablinsky

The beautiful blue building of the **Nakhimov Naval School** is a short walk farther east, where young boys learn to carry on the traditions of the Russian fleet. The battleship **Aurora** is anchored in front of it. The cruiser originally fought during the Russo-Japanese War (1904-05). In October 1917, the sailors mutinied and joined in the Bolshevik Revolution. On the evening of October 24, following the orders of Lenin and the Military Revolutionary Committee, the *Aurora* sailed up the Neva and at 9.45 pm fired a blank shot to signal the storming of the Winter Palace. In 1948, it was moored by the Navy School and later opened as a museum. Various displays include the gun that fired the legendary shot, and the radio room where Lenin announced the overthrow of the Provisional Government to the citizens of Leningrad. The battleship is open 10.30 to 4.30, closed Mondays and Fridays. In front of the *Aurora* are a number of kiosks, one an American-Soviet joint venture that sells souvenirs and other food items for foreign currency.

The **Leningrad Hotel** can be reached by crossing the bridge over the Bolshaya Neva. Here you can have a quick coffee, buffet lunch or dinner (for rubles) at the cafeteria-type restaurant on the ground floor.

Kirov Islands

The northernmost islands on the Petrogradskaya side of the Neva (the right bank), the Kirov, are made up of a number of small islands: the Krestovsky, Yelagin and Workers (formerly Stone). Stone Island Bridge leads from the end of Kirov Prospekt to Workers Island, a popular summer resort area in the days of Peter. Paul I erected the beautiful yellow Stone Island Palace on the eastern part of the island. Today it is filled with holiday centers and sanitoriums. Yelagin Island was owned in the late 18th century by a wealthy aristocrat of the same name. A century later, it became the summer residence of the czars. In 1822, Carlo Rossi built the elegant Yelagin Palace for Alexander I. The Kirov Recreation Park now takes up most of the island, where festive carnivals are held during the White Nights.

The largest island in the group, Krestovsky, houses two stadiums, the Dynamo and the 80,000-seat Kirov. At the end of the island is a Buddhist temple, designed by a Tibetan monk. Nearby is the place where Alexander Pushkin fought his duel; a small obelisk marks the spot where he was mortally wounded. The main attraction is Victory Park (built in 1945 after WW II), with artificial lakes and swimming pools. Leningrad poet Anna Akhmatovah wrote: "Early in the morning, the people of Leningrad went out. In huge crowds to the seashore, and each of them planted a tree up on that strip of land, marshy, deserted. In Memory of that Great Victory Day". The Metro line Moskovsko-Petrogradskaya runs out in this direction, beginning with the stop Petrogradskaya.

The Strelka of Vasilyevsky Island

Vasilyevsky is the largest island in the Neva Delta, encompassing over 4,000 acres. At the eastern tip of the island, known as the Strelka (arrow or spit of land), the Neva is at its widest and branches into the two channels of the Bolshaya and Malaya Neva. The Palace and Workers Bridges span the Bolshaya Neva to the left bank and the Malaya to the Petrogradskaya side. At first Peter chose to build his future city, modeled after Venice, on Vasilevsky Island. But when both sides of the Neva froze over in winter, the island was cut off from the rest of Russia. By the mid-18th century, it was decided to develop the administrative and cultural centers instead on the left bank of the Neva. However, many of the original canals are still present on the island, whose streets are laid out as numbered lines (where canals were planned) and crossed by three major *prospekts*.

After Peter and Paul Fortress was completed, vessels docked along the Strelka. The Exchange Hall was the first wooden building on the Strelka, where merchants and visiting tradesmen gathered. By the end of the century, a stone building was erected to house the new Stock Exchange. Thousands of piles were driven into the riverbed to serve as the foundation for a granite embankment with steps leading to the Neva flanked on each side by two large stone globes. This area served as the main port of the city from 1733 to 1855, before it was switched to the lower left bank of the Neva. Designed by architect Thomas de Thomon, the Stock Exchange, with 44 white Doric columns and the sea-god Neptune in a chariot harnessed to sea horses over the main entrance, took five years to complete. This building, at 4 Pushkin Square, now serves as the **Central Naval Museum,** open 10.30 am–5 pm, closed on Mondays and Tuesdays). Peter originally opened this museum in the Admiralty in 1709 to store models and blueprints of Russian ships. His collection numbered over 1,500 models and the museum contains a half million items on the history of the Russian fleet.

Pushkin Square lies in front of the Exchange. The dark red **Rostral Columns,** 96 feet (32 meters) high, stand on either side of the square. These were also built by de Thomon from 1805 to 1810. The Romans erected columns adorned with the prows of enemy ships, or rostres, after naval victories. These rostral columns are decorated with figures symbolizing the victories of the Russian fleet. Around the base of the columns are four allegorical figures, representing the Neva, Volga, Dnieper and Volkhov rivers. The columns also acted as a lighthouse; at dusk hemp-oil was lit in the bronze bowls at the top. Nowadays, gas torches are used, but only during festivals. This area is one of the most beautiful spots in all of Leningrad, offering a large panoramic view of the city. Imagine the days when the whole area was filled with ships and sailboats. The Frenchman, Alexandre Dumas, was quite captivated with the area on his first visit over a century ago: "I really don't know whether there is any view in the whole world which can be compared with the panorama which unfolded before my eyes".

Two gray-green warehouses, built between 1826 and 1832, stand on either side of the Exchange. The northern warehouse is now the Central Soil Science Museum and the southern the **Zoological Institute and Museum,** which has a collection of over 40,000 animal species, including a 44,000 year-old stuffed mammoth, (both open 11 am–5 pm and closed on Fridays and Saturdays).

The eight-columned **Customs House** (1829-32) along the embankment of the Malaya Neva is topped with mounted copper statues of Mercury (Commerce), Neptune (Navigation) and Ceres (Fertility). The cupola was used as an observation point to signal arriving trade ships. It is now the **Museum of Russian Literature**, generally known as the Pushkin House. In 1905, the Museum purchased Pushkin's library. Other rooms contain exhibits devoted to famous Russian writers such as Lermontov, Gogol, Chekhov, Dostoevsky, Gorky, Blok, Turgenev and Tolstoy. Check before you visit the museum, for it closes now and then for restorative work.

The light green and white **Kunstkammer** (1718-34), with its distinctive domed tower, is located at the beginning of Universitetskaya Naberezhnaya, the University Embankment, which extends west along the Bolshaya Neva. Nearly every building in this district is a monument of 18th-century architecture. Kunstkammer, stemming from the German words *kunst* (art) and *kammer* (chamber), was the first Russian museum open to the public. Legend has it that Peter the Great, while walking along the embankment, noticed two pine trees, entwined around each other's trunks. The czar decided to cut down the trees and build a museum on the spot to house "rarities, curiosities and monsters". The tree was also in the museum. In order to attract visitors, admission was free and a glass of vodka was offered at the entrance. The building became known as the "cradle of Russian science" and was the seat of the Academy of Sciences, founded by Peter in 1724. The famed scientist, Mikhail Lomonosov, worked here from 1741 to 1765. Today the Kunstkammer is made up of the **Ethnographical Institute and Peter the Great Museum** and the **Museum of Mikhail Lomonosov.** In the museum's tower (at the top of the building), the first Russian astronomical observatory was installed. The large globe (nine feet/three meters in diameter) had a model of the heavens in its interior. Twelve people could fit inside, where a mechanism was regulated to create the motion of the night sky, a forerunner of the planetarium. Soon, the Kunstkammer became too small and a new building was constructed next to it for the Academy of Sciences, by the architect, Giacomo Quarenghi, from 1783 to 1788. A statue of Mikhail Lomonosov stands outside the Academy. The museums are open 11 am–5 pm (closed on Fridays and Saturdays).

Peter commissioned the architect, Trezzini, to build the Twelve Collegiums (1722-42) next to the Kunstkammer (along Mendeleyev Prospekt) for his future Senate and Ministries. After 1819, it became part

of St Petersburg University. Many prominent writers and scholars
studied here; Lenin passed his bar examinations and received a degree in
law. Some of the teachers were the renowned scientists, Popov and
Pavlov, and Dmitri Mendeleyev (Periodic Law and Tables) worked here
for 25 years; the apartment where he lived is now a museum. The red and
white buildings are now part of Leningrad University, which has more
than 20,000 students. Higher education is free in the USSR and most
students receive a state stipend.

Adjacent to the University at no. 15 is the yellow baroque-style
Menshikov Palace. Menshikov was the first governor of St Petersburg.
Peter the Great presented his close friend with the whole of Vasilyevsky
Island in 1707. This Palace of Prince Alexander Menshikov, built between 1710 and 1714, was the first stone and residential structure on the
island. It was the most luxurious building in St Petersburg and known as
the Ambassadorial Palace. After the death of Peter the Great, the building was given to the First Cadet Corps as their Military College. The
restored palace is now part of the Hermitage Museum and exhibits
collections of 18th-century Russian culture.

The next building along the embankment, at no. 17, is the **Academy
of Arts** (1764-88). The former Academy of the Three Most Noble Arts

(painting, sculpture and architecture) was founded in 1857 and many of Russia's renowned artists and architects studied here. It is now a museum that depicts the history of Russian art and architecture; open 9.15 am–6 pm, (closed on Mondays and Tuesdays). The largest art school in the world is also here, the Repin Institute of Painting, Sculpture and Architecture.

In front of the Academy, two pink granite **Egyptian Sphinxes** flank the stairway leading down to the water. These 3,000-year-old statues were discovered in the early 19th century during an archaeological excavation on the site of ancient Thebes.

The Lieutenant Schmidt Bridge (a hero of the 1905 Revolution) separates the University Embankment from the Lieutenant Schmidt Embankment. The former Annunciation and Nikolaevsky Bridge (1842-50) was the first permanent bridge across the Neva and is the last bridge crossing the Neva before it flows into the Gulf of Finland. During the White Nights season, it is quite lovely to watch the bridges of the city open at 2 am from this vantage point. The Kirov Cultural Palace is also found here. The rest of the island is largely residential and industrial. The Metro stop closest to the Strelka is Vasiloevstrovkaya.

The Pribaltiiskaya Hotel is at the western end of the island, not far from Metro stop Primorskaya (Maritime). After shopping in the large Beriozka, watch a sunset over the Gulf from the embankment behind the hotel. A few minutes down the road from the hotel is the International Seaman's Club, near the Morskaya Vokzal (Marine Terminal), where most cruiseboats dock. The Olympia Ship, a Swedish hotel and restaurant, offers good meals for foreign currency. Marine Glory Square is in front with permanent glass pavilions that house international exhibitions. The Dekabristov (Decembrist) Island lies farther to the north.

For the next 200 miles (320 kilometers), this section of the Gulf of Finland off Vasilyevsky Island is known as Cyclone Road. West to east, traveling cyclones create what is known as the 'long wave'. Originating in the Gulf during severe storms, it then rolls toward Leningrad. Propelled by high winds, it enters into the narrow banks of the Neva with the speed of a freight train. The city has experienced over 300 floods in its 300-hundred-year history. An 18-mile (29-kilometer) barrier has been built across a section of the Gulf to control the flooding. Much controversy surrounds the barrier, since many scientists believe that it is changing the ecological balance of the area.

The Palace Square

Palace Square was the heart of Russia for over two centuries and is one of the most striking architectural ensembles in the world. It was not only the parade ground for the czar's Winter Palace, but a symbol of the revolutionary struggle as well. The square was, in fact, the site of three revolutions: The Decembrists first held an uprising near here in 1825. On Sunday, January 9, 1905 over 100,000 people marched to Palace Square to protest intolerable working conditions. The demonstration began peacefully as the families carried icons and pictures of the czar. But Nicholas II's troops opened fire on the crowd, and thousands were killed in the event known as "Bloody Sunday". After the massacre, massive strikes ensued. In October of the same year, the ' St Petersburg Soviet of Workers' Deputies' was formed. Twelve years later, in February 1917, the Kerensky Government overthrew the autocracy and in October, the Red Guards stormed through Palace Square to capture the Winter Palace from the Provisional Government.

In 1819, Carlo Rossi was commissioned to design the square. The government bought up all the residential houses and reconstructed the area into the Ministries of Foreign Affairs and Finance, and the General Staff Headquarters of the Russian Army. These two large yellow buildings curve around the southern end of the Square and are linked by the **Triumphal Arch** (actually two arches), whose themes of soldiers and armor commemorate the victories of the War of 1812. It is crowned by the 16-ton Winged Glory in a chariot led by six horses, which everyone believed would collapse the arch. On opening day, Rossi declared: "If it should fall, I will fall with it". He climbed to the top of the arch as the scaffolding was removed.

As you enter Palace Square from Herzen Street, an unforgettable panorama (of the palace and square) unfolds . The Alexander Column stands in the middle of the square, symbolizing the defeat of Napoleon in 1812. Nicholas I had it erected in memory of Alexander I. The 700-ton piece of granite took three years to be extracted from the Karelian Isthmus and brought down by a system of barges to the city. Architect Auguste Montferrand supervised the polishing in 1830, and by 1834 the 143-foot-high (47.5-meter) column was erected by 2,500 men using an elaborate system of pulleys. The statue of the angel (whose face resembles Alexander I) holding a cross was carved by sculptor Boris Orlovsky. The Guard's Headquarters (to the right of the Column facing the Palace) was built by Bryullov (1837-43) and now serves as an administrative building.

The main architectural wonder of the Square is the **Winter Palace**, standing along the banks of the Neva. This masterpiece by Rastrelli was commissioned by the Czarina Elizabeth, daughter of Peter, who, fond of the baroque style, desired a lavish Palace decorated with columns, stucco and sculptures. It was built from 1754 to 1762, as Rastrelli remarked, "solely for the glory of all Russia". The Palace remained the czars' official residence until the February 1917 Revolution. The magnificent Palace extends over 20 acres and the total perimeter measures over a mile (2 kilometers)! There are 1,057 rooms (not one identical), 1,945 windows, 1,886 doors and 117 staircases. The royal family's staff consisted of over 1,000 servants. At 600 feet (200 meters) long and 66 feet (22 meters) high, it was the largest building in all St Petersburg. After the 1837 fire destroyed a major portion of the Palace, architects Bryullov and Stasov restored the interior along the lines of Russian Classicism, but preserved Rastrelli's light and graceful baroque exterior. The blue-green walls are adorned with 176 sculpted figures. The interior was finished with marble, malachite, jasper, semi-precious stones, polished woods, gilded moldings and crystal chandeliers. In 1844, Nicholas I passed a decree (in force until 1905) stating that all buildings in the city (except churches) had to be at least six feet (two meters) lower than the Winter Palace. During WW II, the Winter Palace was marked on German maps as "Bombing Objective no. 9". Today, the Winter Palace houses the **State Hermitage Museum**.

The largest museum in the Soviet Union, the State Hermitage, houses close to 2,800,000 exhibited items, seen by more than three million people annually. It contains one of the largest and most valuable collections of art in the world, dating from antiquity to the present.

Peter the Great began the city's first art collection after visiting Europe. In 1719, Peter I purchased Rembrandt's *David's Farewell to Jonathan*, a statue of Aphrodite (*Venus of Taurida*), and started a museum of Russian antiquities (now on display in the Hermitage's Siberian collection).

In 1764, Catherine the Great created the **Hermitage** (a French word meaning "secluded spot") in the Winter Palace for a place to house 225 Dutch and Flemish paintings she had purchased in Berlin. Her ambassadors were often sent to European countries in search of art; in 1769, she

Code of the

t the entrance of one hall, I found behind a green curtain the social rules of the Hermitage, for the use of those intimate friends admitted by the Czarina into her asylum of Imperial Liberty.

I will transcribe, **verbatim**, this charter, granted to social intimacy by the caprice of the sovereign of the once enchanted place: it was copied for me in my presence:-

RULES TO BE OBSERVED ON ENTERING.

ARTICLE 1
On entering, the title and rank must be put off, as well as the hat and sword.

ARTICLE II
Pretensions founded on the prerogatives of birth, pride, or other sentiments of a like nature, must also be left at the door.

ARTICLE III
Be merry; nevertheless, **break nothing and spoil nothing.**

ARTICLE IV
Sit, stand, walk, do whatever you please, without caring for any one.

ARTICLE V
Speak with moderation, and not too often, in order to avoid being troublesome to others.

Empress Catherine

ARTICLE VI
Argue without anger and without warmth.

ARTICLE VII
Banish sighs and yawns, that you may not communicate ennui, *or be a nuisance to any one.*

ARTICLE VIII
Innocent games, proposed by any members of the society, must be accepted by the others.

ARTICLE IX
Eat slowly and with appetite: *drink with moderation, that each may walk steadily as he goes out.*

ARTICLE X
Leave all quarrels at the door; what enters at one ear must go out at the other *before passing the threshold of the Hermitage. If any member violate the above rules, for each fault witnessed by two persons, he must drink* a glass of fresh water (ladies not excepted): *furthermore, he must read aloud a page of the Telemachiad (a poem by Trediakofsky). Whoever fails during one evening in three of these articles, must learn by heart six lines of the Telemachiad. He who fails in the tenth article must never more re-enter the Hermitage.*

Marquis Astolphe Louis Leonard de Custine, Russia, 1854-5.

purchased the entire collection of Count de Bruhl of Dresden for 180,000 rubles. The Hermitage numbered almost 4,000 paintings at the time of her death. Subsequent czars continued to expand the collection: Alexander I bought the entire picture gallery of Josephine, wife of Napoleon, and Nicholas I even purchased pictures from Napoleon's stepdaughter. Until 1852, the Hermitage was only open to members of the royal family and aristocratic friends. Catherine the Great wrote in a letter to one of her close friends that "all this is admired by mice and myself". A small list of rules, written by Catherine, hung by the Hermitage's entrance: "Make merry, but do not spoil, break or gnaw anything. Eat with pleasure, but drink with measure, so you will be able to find your feet when you go out the door". In 1852, Nicholas I opened the Hermitage on certain days as a public museum (but still closed to common people), and put it under the administrative direction of curators. After the 1917 Revolution, the Hermitage was opened full-time to the whole public.

The Hermitage occupies several other buildings in addition to the Winter Palace. The **Little Hermitage** housed Catherine's original collection in a small building next to the Palace; it was constructed by Vallin de la Mothe in 1764-67. Stakenschneider's Pavilion Hall is decked with white marble columns, 28 chandeliers, the four "Fountains of Tears" and the Peacock Clock. The royal family would stroll in the "hanging gardens", along with peasants and peacocks in the summer. In winter, snow mounds were built for sledding. The **Old Hermitage** (or Large Hermitage) was built right next to it to provide space for Catherine's growing collections. The **Hermitage Theater**, Catherine's private theater, is linked with the Old Hermitage by a small bridge that spreads across the Winter Ditch canal. The theater was built by Quarenghi in 1787 and modeled after the amphitheaters of Pompei. The **New Hermitage** (1839-52), located behind the Old Hermitage, houses additional works of art. Its main entrance off Khalturina Street is composed of the 10 large and powerful **Statues of Atlas**. They were carved by Terebenyer from blocks of granite.

The Hermitage collections span a millennia of art and culture. It is said that if a visitor spent only a half minute at each exhibit, it would take nine years to view them all! A map of the layout can be purchased inside, from which you can select places of interest. Particularly impressive are the Ambassadorial Staircase (at the Neva entrance), Gallery of the War of 1812, the Royal Suites, Throne Room of Peter the Great, Golden Room, Vatican Room, Malachite Room and Hall of St George. Where the Imperial Throne once stood, in St George Hall, now hangs an enormous mosaic map of the Soviet Union covered with 45,000 semi-precious stones. Moscow is marked by a ruby star and Leningrad is written in letters of alexandrite. The 19-ton Kolyvan Vase was made from Altai jasper and took 14 years to carve. An entire wall in the Hermitage was knocked down to bring it inside.

Other exhibits delineate the history of Russian culture on the first floor; primeval art (over 400,000 objects) is covered on the ground floor; oriental art and culture (a quarter-million pieces) from Egypt, Babylon, Byzantium, Middle East, Japan, China and India, occupy the second and ground floors; antique culture and art from Greece, Italy and Rome are also on the ground floor. Over 650,000 items in the collection of the art of Western Europe are found on the first and second floors. This includes paintings by da Vinci, Raphael, Titian, El Greco, Rubens, Rembrandt, and a fine Impressionist collection by Monet, Lautrec, Van Gogh and Picasso. In addition are numerous displays of sculpture, tapestries, china, jewelry, furniture, rare coins and handicrafts. A recommended book to buy at the Hermitage store is *Saved for Humanity*, tracing the history of the museum (with pictures and available in English, German and Russian). The museum is open from 10.30 am–5 pm, Thursday noon-8 pm, closed on Monday. Entrance tickets are sold at kiosks outside the Winter Palace. Or book a tour through the Intourist desk at your hotel.

Leaving the Hermitage through Palace Square to the left and past the Guard's Headquarters brings you through the Choristers' Passage and across a wide bridge known as Pevchesky Most (Singers Bridge). This bridge crosses the lovely **Moika Canal** and leads to the former Imperial Choristers' Capella (1831), now the Glinka Academy Capella. At no. 12 Moika, to the left of the Capella, is the Pushkin Museum, where the poet lived from October 1836 until his death in January 1837. A statue of Pushkin stands in the courtyard. The rooms have all been preserved and contain his personal belongings and manuscripts. The study is arranged in the exact order it was left after Pushkin died on the divan from a wound he received in a duel. Even the clock is set to the moment of his death, 2.45 am. The next room displays the clothes worn during the duel and his death mask. Since Pushkin is still one of the most popular figures in the USSR, museum tickets are often sold out; it may be necessary to buy them a few days in advance. The museum is open 10.30 am–6.30 pm, (Thursdays noon-8 pm, closed on Tuesdays).

The many rooms of The Hermitage.

The Area of Decembrists' Square

Walking west of the Winter Palace along the Neva, you come to another chief architectural monument of the city, the **Admiralty**, recognizable by its long golden spire, topped by a golden frigate, the symbol of Leningrad. The best views of the building are from its southern end. A beautiful fountain stands in the middle of Maxim Gorky Garden surrounded by busts of Glinka, Gogol and Lermontov. In 1704, Peter the Great ordered a second small outpost constructed on the left bank of the Neva and opposite the main part of town. This shipyard was later referred to as the Admiralty. Over 10,000 peasants and engineers were employed to work on the Russian naval fleet. By the end of the 18th century, the Navy had its headquarters here. Whenever the Neva waters rose during a severe storm, a lantern was lit in the spire to warn of coming floods. In 1738, the main building was rebuilt by the architect, Ivan Korobov, who replaced the wooden tower with a golden spire. From 1806 to 1823, the building was again redesigned by Zakharov, an architectural professor at the St Petersburg Academy. The spire was heightened to 218 feet (72.5 meters) and decorated with 56 mythological figures and 350 ornamentations based on the glory of the Russian fleet. The scene over the main-entrance archway depicts Neptune handing over his trident to Peter the Great, a symbol of Peter's mastery of the sea. In 1860, many of the statues were taken down when the Orthodox Church demanded the "pagan" statues removed. Today the Admiralty houses the Dzerzhinsky Naval School.

Across the street from the Admiralty at no. 6 Admiralty Avenue is the building known as the All Russia Extraordinary Commission for Struggle Against Counter-Revolution and Sabotage, the*VeCheKa.* Felix Dzerzhinsky, the first chairman of the Cheka Police Force (forerunner of the KGB), had his office here. His best remembered words were that a member of the Cheka "must have clean hands, a warm heart and a cold head". A memorial museum, dedicated to Dzerzhinsky, has been here since 1974.

Next to the Admiralty, situated right along the Neva, is the infamous Decembrists' Square, formerly known as Senate and Peter Square. In 1925, to mark the 100-year anniversary of the Decembrist uprising, the area was renamed Decembrists' Square. After the Russian victory in the "Patriotic War of 1812" and the introduction of principles from the French Enlightenment, both the nobility and peasants wanted an end to the monarchy and serfdom. An opportune moment for insurrection came on November 19, 1825, when Czar Alexander I suddenly died. A secret revolutionary society, consisting mainly of noblemen, gathered over 3,000 soldiers and sailors who refused to swear allegiance to the new czar, Nicholas I. The members compiled the "Manifesto to the Russian People", which they hoped the Senate would approve. (What they did not know was that the Senate had already proclaimed their loyalty to Nicholas.) They decided to lead an uprising of the people in Senate Square on December 14, 1825 and from there, to capture the Winter Palace and Peter and Paul Fortress. But Nicholas I discovered the plan and surrounded the square with armed guards. The Decembrists marched to an empty Senate and, moreover, Prince Trubetskoi, who was elected to lead the insurrection, never showed up! Tens of thousands of people joined the march and prevented the guards from advancing on the main parties. But Nicholas I then ordered his guards to open direct fire on the crowd. Hundreds were killed and mass arrests followed. In addition, over 100 people were sentenced to serve 30 years in penal servitude. Five leaders of the rebellion were hanged in Peter and Paul Fortress. Others received such sentences as having to run a gauntlet of a thousand soldiers 12 times, amounting to 12,000 blows by rod. Even though the 1825 revolution was unsuccessful, "the roar of cannon on Senate Square awakened a whole generation", observed the revolutionary writer, Alexander Herzen.

In 1768, Catherine the Great commissioned the sculptor, Etienne Falconet, to build a monument to Peter the Great. For 12 years, Falconet worked "to create an alive, vibrant and passionate spirit". He successfully designed a rider on a rearing horse, crushing a serpent under its feet—just as Peter reared St Petersburg. Instead of a molded pedestal, Falconet wanted to place his monument atop natural stone. A suitable rock was found about six miles (10 kilometers) from the city. It had been split by lightning and was known as Thunder Rock. Peter the Great was said to have often climbed the rock to view his emerging city. With the help of levers, the 1,600-ton rock was raised on a platform of logs and rolled to the sea on a system of copper balls; it took a year to get it to St Petersburg. The rock bears the outlines of crashing waves. Marie Collot, Falconet's pupil and future wife, sculpted the head, and the Russian sculptor, Gordeyev, the snake. The bronze inscription on the base, written in Russian and Latin, reads: "To Peter I from Catherine II, 1782", the date the monument was unveiled. The monument to Peter came to be known as **The Bronze Horseman**, after the popular poem by Pushkin.

The nearby yellow-white buildings linked by an arch were built in the 1830s by Carlo Rossi. This ensemble was used as the Senate, Supreme Court and Holy Synod before the Revolution. Today they house the State Historical Archives. Take a stroll down the small Krasnaya Ulitsa, that lies beyond the arch; this was the area of the galley shipyards. The two Ionic columns, standing at the start of the next boulevard, bear the goddesses of Glory. These monuments commemorate the valor of Russia's Horse Guards during the war against Napoleon. The building that looks like an ancient Roman temple, is the Horse Guard Manège, where the czar's horseguards were trained. Today it is used as an exhibit hall for the Union of Artists.

St Isaac's Square

The whole southern end of Decembrists' Square is framed by the grand silhouette of **St Isaac's Cathedral**. In 1710, the first wooden church of St Isaac was built by Peter, who was born on the day which celebrated the sainthood of Isaac of Dalmatia; it was replaced in 1729 by one of stone. At that time, the church was situated nearer to the banks of the Neva, and it eventually began to crack and sink. It was decided in 1768 to build another church farther away from the riverbank. But at its completion in 1802, the church was not deemed grand enough for the growing magnificence of the capital. After the War of 1812, Czar Alexander I announced a competition for the best design of a new St Isaacs. The young architect, Montferrand, presented an elaborate album filled with 24 different variations, from Chinese to Gothic, for the czar to choose from. Montferrand was selected for the monumental task in 1818, and the czar also assigned the architects, Stasov, Rossi and the Mikhailov brothers, to help with the engineering.

The cathedral took 40 years to build. In the first year alone, 11,000 serfs drove 25,000 wooden planks into the soft soil to set a foundation. Each of the 112 polished granite columns, weighing 130 tons, had to be raised by a system of pulleys. The system was so perfected that the monolithic columns were eventually installed in a mere 45 minutes. The entire building weighs over 300,000 tons. The three domes give the cathedral a total height of 305 feet (101.5 meters). An observation deck along the upper colonnade (562 steps to climb) provides a magnificent view of the city. The State spared no expense—the cathedral cost 10 times more than the Winter Palace. Nearly a 100 kilos of pure gold were used to gild the dome, which, in good weather, is visible 25 miles (40 kilometers) away. The interior is faced with 14 different kinds of marble, and 43 other types of stone and minerals. The Foucault pendulum swings down 279 feet (93 meters) from the dome, measuring the rotation of the Earth. Inside at the western portico is a bust of Montferrand, made from each type of marble. (Montferrand died one month after the completion of the cathedral. He had asked to be buried within the walls, but the Czar, Alexander II, refused. Instead, Montferrand was buried in Paris.) It can hold 14,000 people and is filled with over 400 sculptures, paintings and mosaics by the best Russian and European masters of the 19th century. Twenty-two artists decorated the iconostasis, ceilings and walls. The altar's huge stained-glass window is surrounded by frescoes and Bryullov painted the frescoes in the ceiling of the main dome. A St Petersburg newspaper wrote that the cathedral was "a pantheon of Russian art, as artists have left monuments to their genius in it". On May 29, 1858, St Isaac's was inaugurated with much pomp and celebration as the main cathedral of St Petersburg. In 1931, it was opened by the government as a museum, now open 11 am–6 pm daily, except on Wednesdays.

St Isaac's Square, in front of the cathedral, was originally a marketplace in the 1830s. At its center stands the bronze statue of Nicholas I, constructed by Montferrand and Clodt in 1856-59. The czar, who loved horses and military exploits (nicknamed "Nicholas the Stick"), is portrayed in a cavalry uniform wearing a helmet with an eagle. His horse rests only on two points. The bas-reliefs around the pedestal depict the events of Nicholas' turbulent rule. One of them shows Nicholas I addressing his staff after the Decembrist uprising. The four figures at each corner represent Faith, Wisdom, Justice and Might, and depict the faces of Nicholas' wife and three daughters, who commissioned the statue.

The two buildings on each side of the monument were built between 1844-53 and now house the Institutes of the Lenin Academy of Agricultural Sciences. Behind the monument is the **Blue Bridge** (1818), broadest in the city. The structure, even though it appears as a continuation of the square, is actually a bridge over the Moika River. There was a slave market here before the abolition of serfdom in 1861. It is painted blue on the sides facing the water. Many of St Petersburg's bridges were named after the color they were painted; up river are the Green and Red bridges. On one side of the bridge is an obelisk crowned by a trident. Five bronze bands indicate the level of the water during the city's worst floods. The Leningrad poet, Vera Inber, wrote of this place:

"Here in the city, on Rastrelli's marble
Or on plain brick, we see from time to time
A mark: 'The water-level reached this line'
And we can only look at it and marvel".

Beyond the bridge stands the former Mariinsky Palace. It was built in 1839-44 for Maria, the daughter of Nicholas I. In 1894, it was turned into the State Council of the Russian Empire. The artist, Repin, painted the Centennial Gala of the Council in 1901, entitled *The Solemn Meeting of the State Council*; it can be viewed at the Russian Museum. In 1917, the Palace was the residence of the Provisional Government. It now houses the Executive Committee of the Leningrad City Soviet of People's Deputies. The red flag, with a vertical blue stripe, flies on top of the building. The gray seven-story **Astoria Hotel**, on the west side of the square, was built in 1910, one of the grandest hotels in the city. Hitler even sent out engraved invitations for a banquet to be held at the Astoria on November 7, 1942, as soon as he captured the city. Of course, this never took place. The hotel has recently been remodeled and is a very popular place to stay. In front of it is the Lobanov-Rostovsky Mansion. Montferrand built this for the Russian diplomat between 1817 and 1820. Pushkin mentioned the marble lions in front of the house in the *Bronze Horseman*, when the hero climbed one of them to escape the flood. The mansion is referred to as the "House with Lions".

The Gathering Storm

**T**wo centuries had passed like a dream: Petersburg, standing on the edge of the earth in swamp and wilderness, had daydreamed of boundless might and glory; palace revolts, assassinations of emperors, triumphs and bloody executions had flitted past like the visions of a delirium; feeble women had wielded semi-divine power; the fate of nations had been decided in hot and tumbled beds; vigorous strapping young fellows with hands black from tilling the soil had walked boldly up the steps of the throne to share the power, the bed and the Byzantine luxury of queens.

The neighbours looked with horror at these frantic ravings and the Russian people listened in fear and sorrow to the delirium of their capital city. The country nurtured these Petersburg wraiths with its blood but could never sate them.

Petersburg lived a restless, cold, satiated, semi-nocturnal life. Phosphorescent, crazy, voluptuous summer nights; sleepless winter nights; green tables and the clink of gold; music, whirling couples behind windows, galloping troikas, gypsies, duels at daybreak, ceremonial military parades to the whistling of icy winds and the squealing of fifes, before the terrifying gaze of the Byzantine eyes of an Emperor—such was the life of the city.

In the last ten years huge enterprises had sprung into being with unbelievable rapidity. Fortunes of millions of roubles appeared as if out of thin air. Banks, music-halls, skating rinks, gorgeous public-houses of concrete and glass were built, and in them people doped themselves with music, with the reflections of many mirrors, with half-naked women, with light, with champagne. Gambling clubs, houses of assignation, theatres, picture houses, amusement parks cropped up like mushrooms. Architects and business men were hard at work on plans for a new capital city of unheard-of luxury, to be built on an uninhabited island near Petersburg.

An epidemic of suicides spread through the city. The courts were crowded with hysterical women listening eagerly to details of bloody and prurient crimes. Everything was accessible: the women no less than the riches. Vice was everywhere—the imperial Palace was stricken with it as with a plague.

Petersburg, like every other city, had a life of its own, tense and intent. But the central force that governed its movements was not merged with the thing that might be called the spirit of the city. The central force strove to create peace, order and expediency, while the spirit of the city strove to destroy them. The spirit of destruction was everywhere; it soaked everything with its deadly poison, from the stock exchange machinations of the notorious Sashka Sakelman and the sullen fury of the workmen in the steel foundries to the contorted dreams of some fashionable poetress sitting at 5 a.m. in the Bohemian basement café 'Red Jingle'. Even those who would have fought against all this destruction merely increased it and rendered it more acute without knowing it.

It was a time when love and all kindly and healthy feelings were considered in bad taste and out of date. No one loved; but all were thirsty and snatched like men poisoned at everything sharp that would rend their bowels.

Young girls were ashamed of their innocence and married couples of their fidelity to each other. Destruction was considered in good taste and neurosis a sign of subtlety. This was the gospel taught by fashionable authors suddenly emerging from nowhere in the course of a single season. People invented vices and perversions for themselves merely to be in the swim.

Such was Petersburg in 1914. Tormented by sleepless nights, deadening its misery with wine, gold and loveless love, the shrill and feebly emotional strains of tangos for its funeral dirge, the city lived as if in expectation of a fatal and terrible day of wrath. There were auguries in plenty, and new and incomprehensible things were emerging from every cranny.

Alexei Tolstoy, The Road to Calvary, *translated by Edith Bone*

On the other side of the square stands Myatlev's House. Built in 1760 for the poet by Rinaldi, it is one of the oldest structures on the square. Behind the house is the **Museum of Musical Instruments**, with one of the largest collections (3,000) of musical instruments in the world. Some of the items on display are the grand pianos of Rimsky-Korsakov, Glinka and Rubenstein. The museum is open on Wednesdays, Fridays, and Sundays.

Also in the area check out the Intourist Building, originally built in 1910 to accommodate the German Embassy. A short walk away at no. 4 Podbelsky Street is the **Popov Central Communication Museum,** which traces the history of communications in the USSR; open noon-6 pm, closed on Monday. Nearby, at no. 9 Communication Union Street is the General Post Office (1782-89), with the Clock of the World mounted on its archway. Dostoyevsky lived at no. 23 Gogol Street before his imprisonment at Peter and Paul Fortress. Here he wrote *Netochka Nezvanova* and *The White Nights*.

Field Of Mars

A short walk east from the Hermitage, along Khalturin Street (once known as **Millionnaya**, Millionaire's Row), brings you to the **Marble Palace.** In 1785, Catherine the Great commissioned Antonio Rinaldi to build a palace for her favorite (at the time) Count Grigory Orlov. But Orlov died before its completion, and it was turned over to a grand-duke. This was the only building in St Petersburg faced both inside and outside with marble, 32 different kinds. In 1937, the Marble Palace opened as the Leningrad Branch of the Central Lenin Museum (open 10.30 am–6.30 pm, closed on Wednesdays). Over 10,000 exhibits in 34 rooms relate to Lenin's life and work. In Leningrad alone, over 250 places are associated with Lenin. In a small garden at the main entrance stands an armored car with the inscription, "Enemy of Capital". After the February 1917 Revolution, Lenin returned to St Petersburg from exile in Europe in this armored car and, upon his arrival at the Finland Station on April 3, he delivered a speech from the turret proclaiming, "Long live the Socialist Revolution!" On February 22, 1924, the Central Committee declared that "All that is truly great and heroic in the proletariat—a fearless mind, a will of iron—unbending, persistent and able to surmount all obstacles, a revolutionary passion that moves mountains, boundless faith in the creative energies of the masses—all this found splendid embodiment in

Lenin, whose name has become the symbol of the new world from East to West, North to South".

Right in front of the Kirov Bridge is **Suvorov Square**, with the statue of the Russian General, Alexander Suvorov, depicted as the God of War. The square opens to one of the most beautiful places in Leningrad, the Field of Mars. Around 1710, Peter the Great drained the marshy field and held parades after military victories. The festivities ended in fireworks (known in those times as "amusement lights"), so the square was called **Poteshnoye Polye** (Amusement Field). By the end of the 18th century, the area was used as a routine drill field, which destroyed the grasses; for a while the field was nicknamed the " St Petersburg Sahara". When, in 1801, the monument to Field Marshal Suvorov, depicted as Mars, was placed here (it was moved to its present location in Suvorov Square in 1818), the area became known as **Marsovo Polye** (Field of Mars). The 30-acre (12-hectare) field is bordered on the west by the Barracks of the Pavlovsky Regiment, the first among the czar's armies to take the side of the people during the February 1917 Revolution. It is now the Leningrad Energy Commission. The southern side is bordered by the Moika River and Griboyedov Canal, and the eastern by the lovely narrow **Lebyazhya Kanalka** (Swan Canal).

The **Memorial to the Fighters of the Revolution** stands in the center. On March 23, 1917, 180 heroes of the February uprising were buried here in mass graves. The next day, the first granite stone was laid in the monument foundation, which was unveiled in 1920. On each of the eight stone blocks are words by the writer, Anatoly Lunacharsky. One reads: "Not victims, but heroes, lie beneath these stones. Not grief, but envy, is aroused by your fate in the hearts of all your grateful descendants". During the 40th anniversary of the October Revolution in 1957, the eternal flame was lit, in memory of those killed during the revolutions.

The eastern side of the Field opens up on the lovely **Letny Sad** (Summer Garden). The main entrance to the garden is from the Neva-Kutuzov embankment. A beautiful black and golden grille (1770-84 by Yuri Felten) fences it. The open railing, decorated with 36 granite columns and pinkish urns, is one of the finest examples of wrought-iron work in the world. The Summer Garden, the city's oldest, was designed by Leblond in Franco-Dutch style in 1704. Peter the Great desired to create a garden more exquisite than Versailles. On 25 acres of land, he

Siege of Leningrad

"It's now the fifth month since the enemy has tried to kill our will to live, break our spirit and destroy our faith in victory...But we know that victory will come. We will achieve it and Leningrad will once again be warm and light and even gay".

Olga Berggolts, *Leningrad Poet*

For 900 days between 1941 and 1944, Leningrad was cut off from the rest of the Soviet Union and the world by German forces. During this harsh period of World War II, the whole city was linked to the outside world only by air drops and one dangerous ice road, "The Road of Life" (opened only in winter), that was laid across the frozen waters of Lake Ladoga.

The invading Nazis were determined to completely destroy Leningrad, and Hitler's goal was to starve and bombard the city until it surrendered. The directive issued to German command on September 29, 1941 stated: "The Führer has ordered the city of St Petersburg to be wiped off the face of the earth...It is proposed to establish a tight blockade of the city and, by shelling it with artillery of all calibres and incessant bombing, level it to the ground". Hitler was so certain of immediate victory that he even printed up invitations to a celebration party to be held in the center of the city at the Hotel Astoria.

But the Germans did not plan on the strong resistance and incredible resilience of the Leningrad people. For almost three years, the Nazis tried to penetrate the city. All totaled, over 100,000 high-explosive bombs and 150,000 shells were dropped on the city. The suffering was immense: almost one million people starved to death. At one point, only 125 grams (four ounces) of bread were allocated to each inhabitant per day. The winters were severe with no heat or electricity. There are many stories, for example, of mothers collecting the crumbs off streets or scraping the paste off wallpaper and boiling it to feed their hungry children. Tanya Savicheva, an 11-year-old girl who lived on Vasilyevsky Island, kept a diary that chronicled the deaths of her entire family. It ended with the words: "The Savichevs died. They all died. I remained alone". Tanya was later evacuated from Leningrad, but died on July 1, 1944.

Damage to the city was extensive. More than half of the 18th-and 19th-century buildings classified as historical monuments were destroyed; over 30 bombs struck the Hermitage alone. Within one month of the German invasion in June 1941, over one million works of art were packed up by the Hermitage staff and sent by train to Sverdlovsk in the Urals for safekeeping. Other works of art and architecture that could not be evacuated were buried or secretly stored elsewhere within the city. Over 2,000 staff members and art scholars lived in 12 underground air-raid shelters beneath the Hermitage in order to protect the museum and its treasures. Boris Piotrovsky, the Hermitage's former director, lived in one of these shelters and headed the fire brigade. He noted that "In the life of besieged Leningrad a notable peculiarity manifested itself—an uncommon spiritual strength and power of endurance...to battle and save the art treasures created over the millennia by the genius of humanity". Architect Alexander Nikovsky, who also lived in an air-raid shelter, sketched the city during the entire blockade. His pencil and charcoal drawings can be seen today in the Hermitage Department of Prints and Drawings.

The city's outskirts were the worst hit. The palaces of Peter the Great, Catherine II, and Elizabeth I were almost completely demolished. Peter's Palace of Petrodvorets was put to use as a Nazi stable. The Germans sawed up the famous Samson Fountain for wood and took rugs and tapestries into the trenches.

The Soviet author, Vera Inber, was in Leningrad during the Seige. She wrote *the* narrative poem "Polkovo Meridian" about the Pulkovo Astronomical Observatory outside Leningrad, where many scientists were killed when it was struck by an enemy bomb.

Dmitri Shostakovich's *The Seventh Symphony* was composed in Leningrad during the siege and broadcast from the city around the world on August 9, 1942. Shostakovich was a member of the fire-defense unit housed in the Leningrad Conservatory. During bomb attacks, Shostakovich would hurriedly write the Russian letters "BT," which stood for air-raid, on his score before running to his post on the roof of the conservatory.

On January 27, 1944, Leningraders heard the salute of 324 guns to celebrate the complete victory over German troops. Even though most of the buildings, museums, and palaces have now been restored, the citizens of Leningrad will never forget the siege, during which every fourth person in the city was killed. May 9th, a city holiday, is celebrated as Liberation Day. School children take turns standing guard at cemeteries.

Over a half million of the people who died between 1941 and 1943 are buried in mass graves at Piskaryovskoye Cemetery outside Leningrad. Inside the pavilion is a museum dedicated to the Siege of Leningrad. Outside, the Statue of the Motherland stands over an eternal flame. At the base of the monument are inscribed words by Olga Berggolts. The end of the inscription reads: "Let no one forget. Let nothing be forgotten".

planted trees and had hothouses, aviaries, grottos and sculptures placed within. Some of the original statues remain, such as Peace and Abundance, the busts of John Sobiesky (a Polish king), Christina (a Swedish queen), the Roman Empress, Agrippina, and Cupid and Psyche. The Swan Canal dug on the western side was filled with swans and had a tiny boat for Peter's favorite dwarf jester. The garden also had many fountains, depicting characters from Aesop's *Fables*. The water for the fountains was drained from a river on its east side; the river was called **Fontanka**, from the Russian *fontan* (fountain). Pipes made from hollowed logs ran from the Fontanka to a city pool, from which a one-mile (1.6-kilometers) pipeline brought water to the gardens. The Fontanka formed the southern border of the city in the mid-18th century. At this time, the first stone bridge was built where the Fontanka flows into the Neva. It is still known as **Prachechny Most** (Laundry Bridge) because it was located near the Royal Laundry. The gardens received their name from the many festivals that Peter the Great loved to hold in summer; the area became the center of social life in St Petersburg.

Many of the fountains, pavilions and statues were destroyed during the 1777 and 1824 floods. The Summer Garden was open only to nobility until, in the mid-19th century, Nicholas I issued a decree, stating that it would be "open for promenading to all military men and decently dressed people. Ordinary people, such as *muzhiks* (peasants) shall not be allowed to walk through the garden". After the Revolution, the Garden was opened fully to the public.

After the garden was designed, Peter had his **Letny Dvorets** (Summer Palace) built at the northern end by the Neva. After its completion in 1714 by Trezzini, Peter moved from his cottage into the Summer Palace. The modest stone building was decorated with 29 terracotta figures and a weather vane of St George slaying the dragon. Peter lived on the ground floor and his wife, Catherine, on the second. In 1974, it was opened as a museum. The Palace is open 11 am–5.30 pm (closed on Tuesdays and from November 11–April 30).

Behind the Summer Palace is an interesting bronze Monument to Ivan Krylov, the popular Russian fablist, by the sculptor, Clodt, and a playground for children with subjects from Krylov's fables. Nearer to the fountain are the **Chainy Domik** (Tea House), built in 1827 by Ludwig Charlemagne, and Coffee House, which is known as "Rossi's Pavilion", built by Rossi in 1826; recitals are now held here. Walking south toward the Moika River, you come upon the Porphyry Vase, a gift to Nicholas I from the Swedish King, Karl Johann.

Engineer's Castle

Crossing the Moika and continuing along the banks of the Fontanka leads to the **Engineer's Castle**, built in 1797-1800 by the architects, Bazhenov and Brenna, for Czar Paul I. Paul did not like his mother's (Catherine the Great) residence in the Winter Palace, and fearing attempts on his life, he ordered the castle constructed as an impregnable fortress. The "Mikhailovsky Castle" (the archangel, Michael, was Paul's patron saint) was bordered in the north by the Moika, and the east by the Fontanka; two artificial canals, the Resurrection and Church, were dug on the other sides, creating a small island. Drawbridges, protected by cannon, were raised at 9 pm when the czar went to bed. In spite of all this, Paul was strangled 40 days after he moved in on March 11, 1801, by one of his own guards.

In 1822, after a military engineering school was opened, the palace became known as Engineer's Castle. Dostoevsky went to school here from 1837 to 1843 (from age 16), and later lived in 17 different residences throughout the city. After the Revolution, it housed a psychiatric institute and now it is a scientific and naval library. In front of the castle's main entrance is a statue of Peter the Great, erected in 1800 and cast by Rastrelli. The inscription at its base reads: "To great-grandfather from great-grandson", ordered by Paul I.

Not far from the Engineer's Castle, along the Fontanka (no. 3) is the **Leningrad Circus**. The circular building of the **Leningradsky Tsirk** was constructed in 1877 by Kenel. Inside is also the Museum of Circus History and Variety Art (established in 1928), with over 100,000 circus-related items (closed on Saturdays and Sundays).

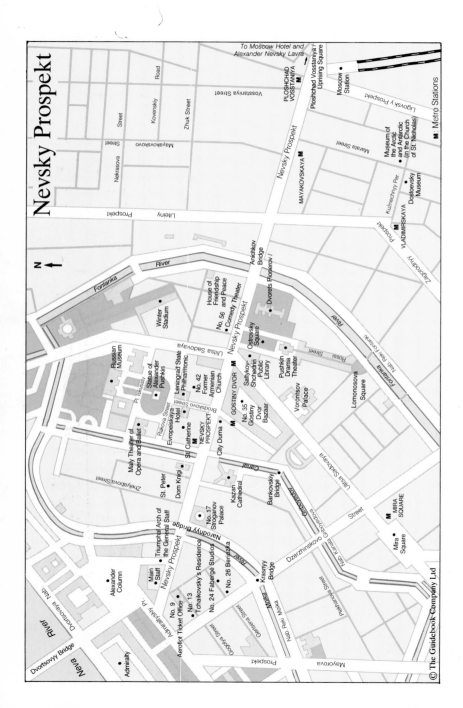

Nevsky Prospekt

N

To Moscow Hotel and
Alexander Nevsky Lavra

PLOSHCHAD
VOSSTANIYA M
Ploshchad Vosstaniya /
Uprising Square

Vosstaniya Street

Moscow
Station

Nevsky Prospekt M

MAYAKOVSKAYA M

Marata Street

Museum of
the Arctic
and Antarctic
(in the Church
of St. Nicholas)

Ligovsky Prospekt

M : Metro Stations

Kuznechny Per

Dostoevsky
Museum

VLADIMIRSKAYA M

Prospekt

Zagorodny

Road

Kovenskiy

Zhuk Street

Street

Mayakovskovo

Street

Nekrasova

Street

Liteiny Prospekt

Fontanka

River

Anichkov
Bridge

House of
Friendship
and Peace

Comedy Theater

No. 56

Dvorets Pioderov /

Winter
Stadium

Nevsky Prospekt

Ostrovsky
Square

Russian
Museum

Statue of
Alexander
Pushkin

Pl. Iskussiv

Ulitsa Sadovaya

No. 42
Former
Armenian
Church

Leningrad State
Philharmonic.

Brodskovo Street

Saltykov-
Shchedrin
Public
Library

Pushkin
Drama
Theater

Rossi Street

River

Fontanka

Nab. Reki Fonanki

Maly Theater of
Opera and Ballet

Rakova Street

Europeiskaya
Hotel

St. Catherine

NEVSKY
PROSPEKT

M

GOSTINY DVOR M

No. 35
Gostiny
Dvor
Bazaar

Vorontsov
Palace

Lomonosova
Square

Zhelyabova Street

St. Peter

Dom Knigi

City Duma

Canal

Kazan
Cathedral

Bankovskiy
Bridge

Ulitsa Sadovaya

Griboyedova

MIRA
SQUARE

M

Mira
Square

Street

Alexander
Column

Main
Staff

Triumphal Arch of
the General Staff

Nevsky Prospekt

Narodny Bridge

No. 17
Stroganov
Palace

Gogolya Street

No. 9

Aeroflot Ticket Office

No. 13

Tchaikovsky's Residence

No. 24 Faberge Studios

No. 26 Berjozka

Gertsena Street

Krasnyy
Bridge

Nab. Reki. Moika

Nab. Kanal Griboyedova

Dzerzhinskovo

Plekhanova Street

Mayorova

Prospekt

Dvortsovy Bridge

Neva

Nab. Admiralteysky Pr.

Admiralty

Dvortsovaya Nab.

River

© The Guidebook Company Ltd

Nevsky Prospekt

In the words of Nikolai Gogol: "There is nothing finer than the Nevsky Prospekt...In what does it not shine, this street that is the beauty of the capital". Nevsky Prospekt, which Leningraders refer to as Nevsky, is the main thoroughfare of the city and the center of business and commercial life. A stroll down part of it, during any time of day, is a must, for no other street like it exists anywhere in the world. It is a busy, bustling area, filled with department stores, shops, cinemas, restaurants, museums, art studios, cathedrals, mansions, theaters, libraries and cafés. The Nevsky is made even more interesting and beautiful by the stunning architectural ensembles that line the three-mile-long (4.8-kilometer) route that stretches from the Admiralty to Alexander Nevsky Monastery. As an architectural showcase, it also brims with history; you can find the spot where Pushkin met his second on the day of his fatal duel, where Dostoevsky gave readings of his works, and where Liszt and Wagner premiered their music.

Shortly after the Admiralty was completed, a track was cut through the thick forest, linking it with the road to Novgorod and Moscow. This main stretch of the city was known as the Great Perspective Road. The road took on the name of Neva Perspectiva in 1738, when it was linked to another small road that ran to Alexander Nevsky Monastery. In 1783, the route was renamed Nevsky Prospekt, the wide, straight road from the Neva to the Nevsky. Peter the Great had elegant stone houses built along the Nevsky and ordered food sold in the streets by vendors dressed in white aprons. The first buildings went up between the Admiralty and the Fontanka Canal. The area, nicknamed "St Petersburg City", was a fashionable place to live, and it became the center for banks, stores and even insurance offices. The architects desired to create a strong and imposing central district and constructed the buildings out of granite and stone brought in from Sweden.

Beginning at the Admiralty (where the street is at its narrowest—75 feet/25 meters), walk along to no. 9 Nevsky. On the corner you will find Vavelberg's House which, originally a bank, is now the Aeroflot ticket office. The large stone house was built in 1912 by the architect, Peretyatkovich, to resemble the Doge's Palace in Venice and the Medici in Florence. At no. 10 across the street is the "Queen of Spades" residence, the house of the old countess on whom Pushkin based his story of the same name. Here the Nevsky is intersected by Ulitsa Gogolya (Gogol

Street), where the writer lived at no. 17 from 1833 to 1836. Here Gogol wrote *Taras Bulba, The Inspector General* and the first chapters of *Dead Souls*. At no. 13 Gogol, Tchaikovsky lived up until his death in 1895.

The next intersection on the Nevsky is Ulitsa Gersena (Herzen Street); Herzen lived at no. 25 for a year in 1840. The main telephone and telegraph center is located to the left by the Triumphal Arch of the General Staff. Fabergé had its main studios at no. 24, and a Beriozka is now at no. 26. The architect, Carlo Rossi, laid out the street along the "Pulkovo Meridian" (which was on the meridian on old Russian maps) so that, at noon, the buildings cast no shadows on the street.

The oldest buildings are at no. 8 and no. 10 Nevsky. Built between 1760 and 1780, they are now exhibition halls for work by Leningrad artists. The house at no. 14 (built in 1939) was once a school. A pale blue rectangular plaque on the wall reads: "Citizens! In the event of artillery fire, this side of the street is the most dangerous!" The House with Columns at no. 15 was built in 1768 as a stage site for one of Russia's first professional theaters. Later a small studio, where Falconet modeled **The Bronze Horseman**, was connected to the theater. It is now the Barrikada Movie Cinema with cafés and shops. The building at no. 18 was known as Kotomin's House (1812-16), after the original owner. Pushkin often frequented the confectioner's shop that used to be in the bottom story; he lived nearby at no. 12 Moika. It was here on January 27, 1837, that Pushkin met up with his second on the way to his fatal duel with George D'ants. The shop is now the **Liternaturnaya Café**, a popular spot to eat that offers piano and violin music. Outside the café, you can have your portrait drawn by one of the numerous artists.

For many years, the section on the left side of the Nevsky beyond the Moika River was reserved for churches of non-Orthodox faiths. The Dutch Church is at no. 20, built in 1837 by Jacquot. The central part functioned as a church and the wings housed the Dutch Mission. The church is now a library. Across the street at no. 17 is the baroque Palace of Count Stroganov, built by Rastrelli in 1754. The Stroganov coat-of-arms is over the gateway arch and depicts two sables and a bear. The Stroganov family owned and developed vast amounts of land in Siberia.

The next intersection is at Zhelyabov Prospekt, named after a popular revolutionary. At no. 13 Zhelyabov is the Rapsodia Music Store; no. 21—the House of Trade, one of the largest department stories in the city; no. 25—Chigorin Chess Club; no. 27—the Leningrad Variety Revue

Theater. Across Zhelyabov Prospekt set back at no. 22-24 Nevsky is the romanesque-style Peter and Paul Lutheran Church, built by Bryullov in 1838. It now belongs to a sports club.

Across the street from the church is the large, majestic, semi-circular colonnade of the **Cathedral of Our Lady of Kazan**. The Kazanski Sobor was named after the famous icon of Our Lady of Kazan that used to be here. It is now on view at the Russian Museum. The architect, Voronikhin, faced two challenges in 1801. First, Czar Paul I wished the cathedral modeled after St Peter's in Rome, and second, the Orthodox Church required that the altar face east, which would have had one side of the cathedral facing the Nevsky. Voronikhin devised 96 Corinthian columns to fan out toward the Nevsky. The bronze Doors of Paradise, which were replicas of the 15th-century Baptisery doors in Florence, opened on the Nevsky side. The structure took 10 years to build and, at that time, was the third largest cathedral in the world. The brick walls are faced with statues and biblical reliefs made from Pudostsky stone, named after the village where it was quarried. The stone was so soft when dug out that it was cut with a saw. It later hardened like rock when exposed to air. In niches around the columns are statues of Alexander Nevsky, Prince Vladimir, St John the Baptist and the Apostle Andrew. The interior was decorated by the outstanding painters Bryullov, Borovikovksy and Kiprensky. There are 56 pink granite columns and polished marble and red-stone mosaic floors. Field Marshall Mikhail Kutuzov is buried in the northern chapel. The general stopped to pray at the spot where he is now buried before going off to the War of 1812. Many trophies from this war, like banners and keys to captured fortresses, hang around his crypt. In 1837, the two statues of Kutuzov and Barclay de Tolly were put up in the front garden.

At the main entrance to the cathedral, to the right off Plekhanov Prospekt, is a small square surrounded by a beautiful wrought-iron grille, called "Voronikhin's Railing". In 1876, the first workers' demonstration took place in front, with speeches by the Marxist, Georgi Plekhanov, (after whom the side street is named). A square and fountain were later added to prevent further demonstrations. But the area remains to this day a popular spot for gatherings and, since *perestroika*, political and religious demonstrations as well. Today the cathedral is the **Museum of the History of Religion and Atheism** (open 11 am–6 pm, closed on Wednesdays).

A short walk down the **Griboyedov Canal** (located to the left behind the cathedral) spans the lovely footbridge of **Bankovski Most** (Bank Bridge), adorned with winged lion-griffins. At the time it was built in 1800, the bridge led to the National Bank; according to Greek mythology, griffins stood guard over gold. On the other side of Nevsky, also on the Griboyedov Canal, is **Dom Knigi**, (House of Books). This polished granite building topped by its distinguishing glass sphere and globe, was originally built by Susor in 1907 for the American Singer Company. The first two floors now make up one of the largest bookstores in the country. The second floor sells posters, calendars and postcards.

The Kazansky Bridge crosses the canal and was built by Illarion Kutuzov, the father of the military leader. Down the canal to the left stands the 17th-century Russian-style building (modeled on St Basil's in Moscow) known as the Savior's Church of Spilled Blood. Spasa Na Krovi was erected on the spot where Czar Alexander II was assassinated in 1881 by a member of the revolutionary group, People's Will. Alexander III ordered architect Alfred Parland, to build the altar where the former czar's blood fell on the cobblestones.

The next building over the bridge at no. 30 was that of the Philharmonic Society, where Wagner, Liszt and Strauss performed. Today it is the Hall of the Glinka Maly Philharmonic. The Catholic Church of St Catherine, built from 1763 to 1783 in baroque-classical design by Vallin de la Mothe, is at no. 32-34 Nevsky. The former Armenian Church, built by Felten in 1780, is at no. 42.

The corner building across the street at no. 31-33 was known as Silver Rows. Built in 1784-87 by Quarenghi, it was used as an open shopping arcade, where silver merchants would set up their wooden display booths. In 1799, the structure was made into the Town Hall or **City Duma**, and a European Rathaus tower was installed. This served as a watch tower, and part of a "mirror telegraph" that linked the residences of the czar. A beam of light was telegraphed along other aligned towers to announce the ruler's arrival or departure.

Right across the street at no. 35 is the **Gostiny Dvor Bazaar**. Visiting merchants used to put up guest houses, *gostiniye dvori*, which served as their resident places of business. From 1761 to 1785, the architect, Vallin de la Mothe, built a long series of open two-tiered arcades, where merchants had their booths. Today the two-story yellow department store, containing over 200 shops, is a popular place for shopping. The small

The Counter-Revolution

N

ow raged the battle of the printing-press—all other weapons being in the
hands of the Soviets.

First, the appeal of the Committee for Salvation of Country and Revolution,
flung broadcast over Russia and Europe;

TO THE CITIZENS OF THE RUSSIAN REPUBLIC

Contrary to the will of the revolutionary masses, on 7 November the
Bolsheviki of Petrograd criminally arrested part of the Provisional
Government, dispersed the Council of the Republic, and proclaimed an
illegal power. Such violence committed against the Government of
revolutionary Russia at the moment of its greatest external danger is an
indescribable crime against the fatherland.

The insurrection of the Bolsheviki deals a mortal blow to the cause of
national defence, and postpones immeasurably the moment of peace so
greatly desired.

Civil war, begun by the Bolsheviki, threatens to deliver the country to
the horrors of anarchy and counter-revolution, and cause the failure of the
Constituent Assembly, which must affirm the republican régime and
transmit to the People for ever their right to the land.

Preserving the continuity of the only legal Governmental power, the
Committee for Salvation of Country and Revolution, established on the
night of 7 November, takes the initiative in forming a new Provisional
Government; which, basing itself on the forces of democracy, will conduct
the country to the Constituent Assembly and save it from anarchy and
counter-revolution. The Committee for Salvation summons you, citizens, to
refuse to recognize the power of violence. Do not obey its orders!

Rise for the defence of the country and the Revolution!

Support the Committee for Salvation!

Signed by the Council of the Russian Republic, the Municipal
Duma of Petrograd, the Tsay-ee-kah (First Congress), the Executive
Committee of the Peasants' Soviets, and from the Congress itself the
Front group, the factions of Socialist Revolutionaries, Mensheviki,

Populist Socialists, Unified Social Democrats, and the group 'Yedinstvo'. *Then posters from the Socialist Revolutionary party, the Mensheviki oborontsi, Peasants' Soviets again; from the Central Army Committee, the Tsentroflot...*

...Famine will crush Petrograd! (they cried). The German armies will trample on our liberty. Black Hundred *pogroms* will spread over Russia, if we all—conscious workers, soldiers, citizens—do not unite...

Do not trust the promises of the Bolsheviki! The promise of immediate peace—is a lie! The promise of bread—a hoax! The promise of land—a fairy tale...

They were all in this manner.

Comrades! You have been basely and cruelly deceived! The seizure of power has been accomplished by the Bolsheviki alone...They concealed their plots from the other Socialist parties composing the Soviet...

You have been promised land and freedom, but the counter-revolution will profit by the anarchy called forth by the Bolsheviki, and will deprive you of land and freedom...

The newspapers were as violent.

Our duty (said the Dielo Naroda) is to unmask these traitors to the working-class. Our duty is to mobilize all our forces and mount guard over the cause of the Revolution!...

Izvestia, *for the last time, speaking in the name of the old Tsay-ee-kah, threatened awful retribution:*

'As for the Congress of Soviets, we affirm that there has been no Congress of Soviets! We affirm that it was merely a private conference of the Bolshevik faction! And in that case, they have no right to cancel the powers of the Tsay-ee-kah...'

Novaya Zhizn, *while pleading for a new Government that should unite all the Socialist parties, criticized severely the action of the Socialist Revolutionaries and the Mensheviki in quitting the Congress, and pointed out that the Bolshevik insurrection meant one thing very clearly: that all illusions about coalition with the bourgeoisie were henceforth demonstrated vain...*

What few Cadet organs appeared, and the bourgeoisie, generally, adopted a detached, ironical attitude towards the whole business, a sort of contemptuous 'I told you so' to the other parties. Influential Cadets were to be seen hovering around the Municipal Duma, and on the outskirts of the Committee for Salvation. Other than that, the bourgeoisie lay low, abiding its hour—which could not be far off. That the Bolsheviki would remain in power longer than three days never occurred to anybody—except perhaps to Lenin, Trotsky, the Petrograd workers, and the simpler soldiers...

John Reed, Ten Days That Shook the World

Statue of Alexander Pushkin in the Square of Arts

building that stands between the Hall and Gostiny Dvor was built as the Portico, and now holds the Central City Theater Booking Office. The art nouveau **Evropeiskaya Hotel** is located across the street from the City Duma on the corner of Nevsky and Brodsky, named after the Soviet painter, Issak Brodsky. The popular hotel, built in the 1870s, was formerly called the Hotel de l'Europe, and has recently been renovated. Two popular cafés are on the ground floor; the Sadko Restaurant serves delicious lunches and dinners.

Across the street, on the next corner, is the Leningrad State Philharmonic Society's Great Hall, built in 1839 by Jacquot for the Club of the Nobility. The St Petersburg Philharmonic Society was founded in 1802. The works of many Russian composers, such as Glinka, Rachmaninov, Rimsky-Korsakov and Tchaikovsky, were first heard at the Society. Wagner was the official conductor during the 1863 season. The Philharmonic Symphony Orchestra performs world-wide. The Philharmonic was named after Dmitri Shostakovich in 1976. Shostakovich lived in Leningrad during the 900-day seige of Leningrad. In July 1941, he began to write his *Seventh Symphony*, while a member of an air-defense unit. Hitler had boasted that Leningrad would fall by August 9, 1942. On this day, the *Seventh* or *Leningrad Symphony*, conducted by Karl Eliasberg, was played in the Philharmonic and broadcast throughout the Soviet Union and the world. "I dedicate my *Seventh Symphony* to our struggle with fascism, to our forthcoming victory over the enemy, and to my native city, Leningrad".

Pushkin Theater (above); Gastronom No 1, Nevsky Prospekt (below)

The square in front of the Philharmonic is called **Ploshchad Iskusstv** (Square of Arts). In the mid-18th century, Carlo Rossi designed the square and the areas in between the Griboyedov Canal, the Moika River and Sadovaya Ulitsa (Garden Street); Garden Street leads past the Winter Stadium and Manège Square to the Engineer's Castle and Field of Mars. The center of the square is dominated by the **Statue of Alexander Pushkin**, sculpted by Mikhail Anikushin in 1957. To the right of the Philharmonic, along Rokov Street, is the Theater of Musical Comedy, the only theater in the city that stayed open during the seige. Next to it is the Komissarzhevskaya Drama Theater. Headed by Russian actress, Vera Komissarzhevskaya, from 1904 to 1906, the company staged plays (including Gorky's) around the political mood of the times.

Behind the square on Engineer's Street stands the majestic eight-columned building of the **Russian Museum**, second largest museum of art in the city. Carlo Rossi built this palace (1819-1827) for Mikhail, youngest son of Paul I; it was called the Mikhailovsky Palace. A splendid wrought-iron fence (embossed by the double-headed eagle) separates the palace from the square. The courtyard allowed carriages to drive up to the front portico, where a granite staircase, lined with two bronze lions, leads to the front door. The Hall of White Columns was so admired by the czar that he ordered a wooden model made for King George IV of England. Rubenstein opened the city's first music school in the hall in 1862. The Mikhailovsky Gardens are situated behind the museum. In 1898, Alexander III set up the Russian Museum inside the palace. The 1,000-year history of Russian art is represented by over 300,000 works of art in the 130 halls of the museum (open 10 to 6, closed on Tuesday). To the right of the museum is the **Museum of Ethnography of the Peoples of the USSR** (also open 10 am–6 pm, closed on Mondays).

The statue of Pushkin gestures to the building in the square known as the **Maly Theater of Opera and Ballet**. Built in 1833 by Bryullov, it was known as the Mikhailovsky Theater, and housed a permanent French troupe. Today it is "the laboratory of Soviet opera and ballet", presenting 360 performances a year in a daily alternating repertory of opera and ballet. Subsidized by the government, it employs nearly 800 people, including an orchestra of 100 and a chorus of 65. It is the second most popular theater (next to the Kirov) in Leningrad. The **Brodsky Museum-Flat**, where many of the artist's paintings are displayed, is next to the Maly; open 11 am–7 pm, closed on Mondays and Tuesdays.

Continuing down the Nevsky, the Saltykov-Shchedrin Public Library stands on the corner of Nevsky and Garden streets. Built in 1801 by Yegor Sokolov, it opened in 1814 as the Imperial Public Library. In 1832, Carlo Rossi built further additions. The statue of Minerva, Goddess of Wisdom, stands atop the building. It is one of the largest libraries in the world—over 25 million books! A reading room is inside, but no books are allowed to be checked out.

The library faces Ostrovsky Square, named after the playwright, Alexander Ostrovsky. A **Statue of Catherine the Great** graces the center; Catherine, dressed in a long flowing robe, stands on a high rounded pedestal that portrays the prominent personalities of the time: Potemkin, Suvorov, Rumyantsev and Derzhavin, to name a few. The square is surrounded by artists' booths with sketches and paintings for sale. Along the left side are two classical pavilions, designed by Rossi, in the Garden of Rest.

Behind the square is the **Pushkin Drama Theater**, a place that looks like a temple to the arts. Flanked by Corinthian columns, the niches are adorned with the Muses of Dance, Tragedy, History and Music. The chariot of Apollo, patron of the arts, stands atop the front façade. The yellow building, erected by Rossi in 1828, was known as the Alexandrinsky Theater (after Alexandra, the wife of Nicholas I), which housed Russia's first permanent theater group. Today it has a varied repetoire of classical and modern plays. Behind the theater is the State Museum of Drama and Music at no. 6 Ostrovsky Square, exhibiting the history of Russian drama and musical theater. It is open 11 am–6 pm, Wednesdays 2 pm–8 pm, Saturdays 11 am–4 pm, closed on Sundays and Tuesdays. The Lunacharsky National Library is also here, with more than 350,000 volumes.

The famous **Rossi Street** (named after the architect) stretches from Ostrovsky to Lomonosov Square. The street has perfect proportions: 68 feet (22 meters) wide, the buildings are 22 meters high and the length is 10 times the width. The world-renowned **Vagonova School of Choreography** is the first building on the left. Twelve boys and 12 girls (children of court servants) were the city's first ballet students, attending a school started by the Empress Anna in the same year, 1768, that she founded the St Petersburg Imperial Ballet. The choreography school now bears the name of Agrippina Vagonova, who taught here from 1921 to 1951. Some of the Imperial Ballet and Vagonova pupils have been Pavlova, Ulanova,

Overdressed

He was so badly dressed that even a man accustomed to shabbiness would have been ashamed to be seen in the street in such rags. In that quarter of the town, however, scarcely any short coming in dress would have created surprise. Owing to the proximity of the Hay Market, the number of establishments of bad character, the preponderance of the trading and working class population crowded in these streets and alleys in the heart of Petersburg, types so various were to be seen in the streets that no figure, however queer, would have caused surprise. But there was such accumulated bitterness and contempt in the young man's heart that, in spite of all the fastidiousness of youth, he minded his rags least of all in the street. It was a different matter when he met with acquaintances or with former fellow students, whom, indeed, he disliked meeting at any time. And yet when a drunken man who, for some unknown reason, was being taken somewhere in a huge wagon dragged by a heavy dray horse, suddenly shouted at him as he drove past: 'Hey there, German hatter!' bawling at the top of his voice and pointing at him—the young man stopped suddenly and clutched tremulously at his hat. It was a tall round hat from Zimmerman's, but completely worn out, rusty with age, all torn and bespattered, brimless and bent on one side in a most unseemly fashion. Not shame, however, but quite another feeling akin to terror had overtaken him.

'I knew it,' he muttered in confusion, 'I thought so! That's the worst of all! Why, a stupid thing like this, the most trivial detail might spoil the whole plan. Yes, my hat is too noticeable... It looks absurd and that makes it noticeable... With my rags I ought to wear a cap, any sort of old pancake, but not this grotesque thing. Nobody wears such a hat, it would be noticed a mile off, it would be remembered...What matters is that people would remember it, and that would give them a clue. For this business one should be as little conspicuous as possible... Trifles, trifles are what matter! Why, it's just such trifles that always ruin everything...'

Fyodor Dostoevsky, Crime and Punishment,
translated by Constance Garnett

Petipa, Nijinsky, Fokine and Balanchine. Over 2,000 hopefuls apply to the school each year, only 90 are chosen. The school's 500 pupils hope to go on to a professional ballet company such as the Kirov. A museum inside the school to the left contains many magical displays, for example Pavlova's ballet shoes and Nijinsky's costumes. Posters and pictures trace the history of ballet from Diaghliev to Baryshnikov who, along with Natalia Makarova, attended the Vagonova School. (The museum is closed to the general public—but if you express an interest in ballet, you may get in.) A few documentary films have been made about the school, such as *The Children of Rossi Street.* The National Geographic Special, *Voices of Leningrad*, available in video rental stores, includes a segment about the Vagonova.

Back on the *prospekt* in the corner building across the street is the impressive **Gastronom no. 1**. Once known as Yeliseyev's, it was the most luxuriant food store in St Petersburg. Today, even though the food supplies have dwindled, it is well worth seeing the interior of the store. The State Puppet Theater, started in 1918, is at no. 52 Nevsky. The Comedy Theater, founded in 1929, is at no. 56. At the corner of Nevsky and the Fontanka River is the House of Friendship and Peace. A former residence, built in the 1790s, it is now a society that promotes friendship and cultural relations with over 500 organizations in 30 countries.

The area around the Fontanka River (the old southern border of the city) was first developed by an engineer team headed by Mikhail An-ichkov, who built the first bridge (still named after him) here in 1715 across the Fontanka. In 1841, a stone bridge with four towers replaced the wooden structure. Peter Klodt cast the tamed-horse sculptures a century ago and today they give the bridge its distinguishing mark. During World War II, the sculptures were buried in the Palace of Young Pioneers across the street. The **Anichkov Bridge** is a popular hang out, and boats to the left on the Fontanka leave frequently for a city tour of the canals and waterways. A kiosk by the dock provides time departures and tickets (sold in rubles only).

The first palace built on the Nevsky was named after Anichkov. Empress Elizabeth (Peter's daughter) commissioned the architects, Dmitriyev and Zemtsov, to build a palace on the spot where she stayed on the eve of her coronation. In 1751, Elizabeth gave the Anichkov Palace to her favorite, Count Alexei Razumovsky. Later, Catherine the Great gave it to her own favorite, Count Grigory Potemkin, who frequently held elaborate balls here. After that it was a part of His Majesty's Cabinet. Since 1937, it has been the **Dvorets Pionerov** (Palace of Young Pioneers). The Young Pioneers is a communist organization for children from ages 9 to 14, who wear distinguishing orange silk scarves to mark their membership. Nearly 15,000 children in the city voluntarily participate in some 600 youth clubs (roughly equivalent to our scouting organizations). The Communist Party Headquarters is at no. 41 Nevsky, originally a mansion built in the 1840s by the architect, Stackenschneider, for a prince by the name of Beloselsky-Belozersky. The Gostiny Dvor/ Nevsky Prospekt Metro stop brings you right out on Nevsky Prospekt by the department store and Dom Knigi. For a list of shops along the Nevsky, see the Practical Information Section.

Following the Nevsky a bit farther (there is little of architectural interest in between), you come to **Ploshchad Vosstaniya** (Uprising Square), named when troops of the czar refused to shoot a group of unarmed demonstrators during the February 1917 uprising. One of the interesting buildings on the Square is **Moskovsky Vokzal** (Moscow Train Station). It was built by the architect, Thon, in 1847. The St Petersburg-Moscow railway line opened on November 1, 1851. A smaller version of this station in Moscow is appropriately named the Leningrad Station. The station was originally planned to contain just shops and galleries surrounded by gardens. The word *vokzal* continued to be used for a station and now Leningrad has five major train *vokzals* in the city: Moscow, Finland, Warsaw, Baltic and Vitebsky. The latter was known as "Czarskoye Selo", the station connecting Russia's first railroad line, built in 1837, to the czar's summer residence in Pavlovsk. The Hotel Oktyabrskaya dates from the 1890s. The Metro stop, Ploshchad Vosstaniya/Mayakovskaya, is near Uprising Square. The Mayakovskaya exit lets you out at about no. 100 Nevsky and Marata Street.

A few blocks down Marata Street from Nevsky is the Marata Banya complex; open 7 am—11pm, closed on Mondays and Tuesdays. At no. 24 Marata is the **Museum of the Arctic and Antarctic** (in the Church of St Nicholas). It is open 10 am– 6 pm, closed on Mondays and Tuesdays.

The modern Moscow Hotel (with restaurants and a Beriozka) stands at the end of Nevsky Prospekt on Alexander Nevsky Square. Across the street is the **Alexander Nevsky Lavra**, the oldest monastery in Leningrad. Peter the Great founded the monastery, southeast of the city, in 1710 and dedicated it to the Holy Trinity and military leader, Alexander Nevsky, Prince of Novgorod, who won a major victory on the Neva (supposedly near the spot of the monastery) against the Swedes in 1240. In Russia, the name *lavra* was applied to a large monastery. Before the Revolution, there were four prestigious *lavra* in the country. The Alexander Nevsky was in St Petersburg; another was the Trinity-St Sergius Monastery in the Golden Ring town of Zagorsk. The Blagoveshchevsky Sobor (Annunciation Church) is the oldest church in the Lavra, built by Trezzini in 1720. It now houses the Museum of Urban Sculpture; open 11 am–6pm, closed on Thursdays.

The Troitsky Sobor (Holy Trinity Cathedral) is the main church of the complex, with a lovely interior, built by Ivan Starov in 1790. The Church of Alexander Nevsky is on the upper floor. In 1723, the remains of Alexander Nevsky himself were brought to the Cathedral. The sarcophagus, cast from 1.5 tons of silver, is now at the Hermitage. Peter the Great buried his sister, Natalie, in the Lazarevskoye Cemetery (to the left of the main entrance), Leningrad's oldest cemetery. To the right of the main entrance is the Tikhvinskoye Cemetery. Here are the beautifully carved gravestones of many of Russia's greatest figures such as Tchaikovsky, Glinka, Rimsky-Korsakov, Mussorgsky, Stasov, Clodt and Dostoevsky. Another entrance is right across the street from the Moscow Hotel. The cemeteries are closed on Thursday and Saturday. The cathedral holds services, and on Alexander Nevsky Day, September 11-12, huge processions take place. Near the monastery is the Theological Seminary, re-established in 1946, which trains 440 students for the clergy. About 100 women are taught to be teachers or choir conductors. Four cathedrals and 18 churches currently perform services in Leningrad. The Alexander Nevsky Bridge, largest bridge in the city, crosses the Neva from the monastery.

Metro stop, Ploshchad Aleksandra Nevskovo, brings you right to the Moscow Hotel and the Monastery complex.

Finland Station

The **Finland Railway Station** is located on the right bank of the Neva, a little east of where the cruiser, *Aurora,* is docked. It is also a short walk from the **Liteiny** (Foundry) **Most** on the Petrogradskaya side, with its beautiful railings filled with mermaids and anchors. The station, behind a towering monument to Lenin, dates back to 1870; from here Lenin secretly left from Petrograd for Finland in August 1917, after he was forced into hiding by the Provisional Government. A few months later he was brought back via the same locomotive to direct the October uprising. This locomotive, engine no. 293, is on display behind a glass pavilion in the back of the station by the platform area. A brass plate on the locomotive bears the inscription: "The government of Finland presented this locomotive to the government of the USSR in commemoration of journeys over Finnish territory made by Lenin in troubled times. June 13, 1957".

The monument to Lenin stands in Lenin Square. After the February 1917 Revolution overthrew the czarist monarchy, Lenin returned to Petrograd from his place of exile in Switzerland on April 3, 1917. He gave a speech from the turret of the car (now on display at the Lenin Museum) to the masses. Originally the Lenin monument was erected on the spot where he gave the speech. But during the construction of the square, the statue, portraying Lenin standing on the car's turret addressing the crowd with an outstretched hand, was moved closer to the Neva embankment, where it stands today. It was unveiled on November 7, 1926. Metro stop, Ploshchad Lenina, lets out at Finland Station.

Crossing the Liteiny Most in front of the station leads to Voinova Prospekt and the Taurida Palace at no. 47. The street was named after Ivan Voinov, who worked as a correspondent for *Pravda* and was killed in this street on July 6, 1917. The palace was built by Ivan Starov in 1789 for Prince Grigory Potemkin—a gift from Catherine the Great. Potemkin was Commander-In-Chief of the Russian Army in the Crimea during the Turkish wars. The peninsula there was called Taurida, and Potemkin was given the title, Prince of Taurida. One party Potemkin held in the palace (costing 200,000 rubles) used 140,000 lamps and 20,000 candles. After both he and Catherine the Great died, the new Emperor Paul I (who disliked his mother, Catherine, and her favorites), converted the palace into a riding house and stables. It was later renovated and became the seat of the State Duma in 1906. On February 27, 1917, the left wing of the palace held the first session of the Petrograd Soviet of Workers.

Lenin—Leader of the Russian Revolution

Lenin, founder of the first Soviet State, was born Vladimir Ilyich Ulyanov, on April 22, 1870. Vladimir, along with his five brothers and sisters, had a strict but pleasant childhood in the small town of Simbirsk (now Ulyanovsk) on the Volga River. On March 1, 1887, when Vladimir was 17, a group of students attempted to assassinate Czar Alexander III in St Petersburg. Vladimir's older brother, Alexander, was one of five students arrested. They were imprisoned in Peter and Paul Fortress in St Petersburg, and on May 8 were hung in the Fortress of Schlüsselburg (Kronstadt).

As a marked family of a revolutionary, the Ulyanovs left Simbirsk for Kazan, where Vladimir attended Kazan University. In December 1887, after the local papers reported the news of the student riots in Moscow, 99 Kazan students protested against the strict rules of their university. Ulyanov, one of them, was immediately expelled and exiled to the town of Kokushkino and kept under police surveillance. Here Vladimir began to study the works of Karl Marx *(Das Kapital,* and *The Communist Manifesto)* and Chernyshevsky *(What Is To Be Done?).* Thereupon, he decided to devote his life to the revolutionary struggle. Lenin wrote that "my way in life was marked out for me by my brother".

Since he was refused permission to enter another university, the young Ulyanov covered the four-year law course, independently, in a little over a year. He then journeyed to St Petersburg and passed the bar exam with honors. With his law degree, Ulyanov moved to the Asian town of Samara, where he defended the local peasants and secretly taught Marxist philosophy.

In 1893, he left again for St Petersburg, where he formed the revolutionary organization, the "League of Struggle for the Emancipation of the Working Class". At 24, in 1894, Vladimir Ulyanov published his first book, *What Are The Friends of the People?* During a secret meeting of the League of Struggle, Ulyanov decided to publish an underground newspaper called *The Workers' Cause.* That same day he was arrested by the police, along with hundreds of other people from the League. Ulyanov was exiled to Siberia, as was Nadezhda Konstantinovna Krupskaya. They were married in the small village of Shushenskoye on July 22, 1898.

While in exile, the League planned the first party newspaper, called *Iskra* (Spark), inspired by words from a Decembrist poem, "A spark will kindle a flame". After the Ulyanov's release, they settled in the town of Pskov outside St Petersburg. Since it was illegal to disseminate any print media criticizing the government, they eventually moved abroad. The first issues of *Iskra* were published in Leipzig, Germany. During these years abroad, Ulyanov wrote books on politics, economics and the revolutionary struggle. In December 1901, Vladimir Ulyanov began signing his writings with the name of Lenin.

In 1903, the Russian Party Congress secretly gathered in London. During this meeting, the Social Democratic Workers Party split into two factions: the Bolsheviks (Majority) and the Mensheviks (Minority). After the session, Lenin led the Bolsheviks to the grave of Karl Marx and said, "Let us pledge to be faithful to his teachings. We shall never give up the struggle. Forward, comrades, only forward".

By 1905, widespread unrest was sweeping across Russia. A popular May Day song was often sung: "Be it the merry month of May. Grief be banished from our way. Freedom songs our joy convey. We shall go on strike today". Workers at the Putilov factory in St Petersburg began a strike that triggered work stoppages at over 350 factories throughout the city. On Sunday, January 9, 1905, thousands of workers lined the streets of St Petersburg. In a peaceful protest, the crowd carried icons and portraits of the Czar. The procession walked toward the Winter Palace and congregated in Decembrist Square. The Palace Guards opened fire. More than 1,000 demonstrators were massacred in what is known today as "Bloody Sunday". Not long afterward, sailors manning the *Potemkin*, largest battleship in the Russian Navy, also protested against their miserable working conditions. In a mutiny headed by Afanasy Matyushenko, the sailors raised their own revolutionary red flag on June 14, 1905.

The Geneva newspapers carried the news of "Bloody Sunday" and Lenin decided to return to St Petersburg. He wrote in his newspaper *Vperyod* (Forward): "The uprising has begun force against force. The Civil War is blazing up. Long live the Revolution. Long live the Proletariat". But it was still too dangerous for Lenin to remain in Russia. Two years later he left again for the West, and over the next ten years, lived in Finland, Sweden, France and Switzerland.

Accounts of a new Russian Revolution were published throughout the West in February, 1917. Lenin immediately took a train to Finland and on April 3 proceeded in an armored car to Petrograd. Today the train's engine is displayed at Leningrad's Finland Station, where Lenin first arrived.

In Petrograd, Lenin lived on the banks of the Moika River and started up the newspaper *Pravda* (Truth), which was outlawed by the new Kerensky Provisional Government. Lenin was later forced into hiding outside the city on Lake Razliv. The hut and area where he hid out has been made into a museum. With his beard shaved off and wearing a wig, Lenin was known as Konstantin Ivanov.

On the grounds of the Smolny Cathedral, a finishing school served as headquarters for the Petrograd Workers Soviet, which organized the Red Guards. During the summer of 1917, more than 20,000 workers in Petrograd were armed and readied for a Bolshevik uprising. Lenin gave the command for attack from the Smolny on October 24, 1917.

To signal the beginning of the Great October Socialist Revolution, the battleship *Aurora* fired a blank shot near the Hermitage. The Red Guards stormed the Winter Palace and almost immediately defeated the White Guards of the Provisional Government; the Moscow Kremlin was taken two days later.

On October 25th, the Second Congress of Soviets opened in the Smolny and Lenin was selected chairman of the first Soviet State; Trotsky was his Foreign Minister. Sverdlov, Stalin, Bobnov and Dzerzhinsky (later to head the Cheka, which authorized police to "arrest and shoot immediately all members of counterrevolutionary organizations") were elected to the Revolutionary Military Committee. Lenin introduced a Decree on Land, proclaiming that all lands become State property. At the end of the Congress, all members stood and sang the *Internationale*, the Proletarian anthem: "Arise ye prisoners of starvation. Arise ye wretched of the earth. For Justic thunders condemnation. A better world's in birth". On March 11, 1918, Lenin moved the capital from Petrograd to Moscow. He lived in a room at the National Hotel across from Red Square. The Bolsheviks, now known as the Communist Party, had their offices in the Kremlin.

During the last years of Lenin's life, the country was wracked by war and widespread famine. He implemented the NEP (New Economic Policy) that allowed foreign trade and investment, but he did not live long enough to bear witness to its effects. Lenin died, at the age of 54, on January 21, 1924. The cause of death was listed as cerebral sclerosis triggered, as stated in the official medical report, by "excessive intellectual activity". In three days a mausoleum was built for him on Red Square. Later, it was replaced by a mausoleum of red granite and marble. Thousands visit this mausoleum daily on Red Square to view his embalmed body and the changing of the guard. Soon after his death, the city of Petrograd's name was changed to Leningrad in his honor.

The father of the Union of Soviet Socialist Republics is seen everywhere throughout the country. Monuments stand in every city, streets and libraries bear his name and his picture is displayed on everything from posters to pins. There is even a Baby Lenin pin (picture of Lenin as a baby) that is presented to young children every October. Both Moscow and Leningrad have their own Lenin Museums. In Leningrad alone over 270 designated memorial spots are associated with the life and work of Lenin.

After Lenin returned to Petrograd in April, he addressed the Congress here on many occasions. Today it houses the Higher Party School and Party conferences. Behind the mansion are the Taurida Gardens and a small children's amusement park. The Russian poet, Derzhavin, wrote of the palace, "Its exterior does not dazzle the eye with carving, gilt or other sumptuous decorations. Its merit is in its ancient, refined style; it is simple, but majestic".

Behind the gardens is the **Museum to Alexander Suvorov,** the great Russian military leader from the War of 1812; open 11 am–6 pm, closed on Wednesdays. Across the street from the front of the palace is the **Kikin Palace.** Built in 1714 and one of the oldest buildings in the city, it belonged to the Boyar Kikin, who plotted, along with Peter's son, Alexei, to assassinate Peter the Great. After Kikin was put to death, Peter turned the palace into Russia's first natural science museum. The collections were later moved to the Kunstkammer on Vasilyevsky Island. Today the yellow-white palace is a children's music school. The closest Metro stop is Chernyshevskaya.

The Smolny

Voinova Prospekt ends at Rastrelli Square, by the monument to Felix Dzerzhinsky. Behind it, the baroque, five-domed, turquoise and white Smolny complex is truly one of Rastrelli's greatest works. Several years after Peter and Paul Fortress was founded, the tar yards, *smolyanoi dvor*,were set up at the Neva's last bend before the Gulf to process tar for the shipyards. Empress Elizabeth, Peter's daughter, wanted to establish a St Petersburg nunnery, and commissoned Rastrelli to build the Smolny Resurrection Convent on this bend. After Elizabeth died, the complex was never fully completed. (Elizabeth lavishly spent State funds; she had over 15,000 gowns. At her death, only six rubles were left in the treasury.) Vassily Stasov later completed the structure in the 1830s, keeping Rastrelli's original design. (When the new classicism vogue in architecture replaced baroque, Rastrelli fell into disfavor under Empress Catherine the Great and was asked to leave the country.)

Catherine set up the Institute for Young Noble Ladies in the Smolny Convent, Russia's first school for the daughters of nobility. Today the Church of the Resurrection and the former convent is the Museum for Leningrad Today and Tomorrow and the Museum of the History of the Leningrad Party; open 11 am—6 pm, closed on Wednesdays. In 1806-08,

Quarenghi erected additional buildings for the Smolny Institute to the right of the convent. In August, 1917, the closed Institute became the headquarters for the Petrograd Bolshevik Party and the Military Revolutionary Committee. On October 25, 1917, Lenin arrived at the Smolny and gave the command for the storming of the Winter Palace. On October 26, the Second All-Russia Congress of Soviets gathered in the Smolny's Assembly Hall to elect Lenin the leader of the world's first "Socialist Government of Workers and Peasants", and to adopt Lenin's Decrees on Peace and Land. John Reed wrote in his book *Ten Days That Shook the World* that Lenin was "unimpressive, to be the idol for a mob, loved and revered as perhaps few leaders in history have been. A leader purely by virtue of intellect; colorless, humorless, uncompromising and detached, without picturesque idiosyncrasies—but with the power of explaining profound ideas in simple terms...he combined shrewdness with the greatest intellectual audacity". Lenin lived at the Smolny for 124 days before transferring the capital to Moscow. Today the places in the Smolny where Lenin lived are part of the Lenin Museum. The rest of the building houses the seat of the Leningrad Regional and City Committees of the Communist Party.

Two pavilions form the main entrances to the building. Each bears an inscription: "Soviet of Proletarian Dictatorship" and "Workers of All Countries, Unite!" A bronze monument of Lenin was set up on the 10th anniversary of the Revolution. A wide avenue leads from the Smolny Institute to Proletarian Dictatorship Square; busts of Karl Marx and Frederick Engels stand on either side of the avenue.

Theater Square

In the southwest part of the city along Glinka and Decembrists prospekts lies **Teatralnaya Ploshchad** (Theater Square). This section of land was once the location for St Petersburg carnivals and fairs. In the 18th century, it was known as *Ploshchad Karusel* (Merry-Go-Round Square). A wooden theater was built here and later, in 1783, it was replaced by the Bolshoi Stone Theater, with over 2,000 seats. In 1836, the drama troupe moved to the Pushkin Theater and the opera remained at the Bolshoi. In 1860, Albert Kavos completed the Mariinsky Theater (which replaced the Bolshoi), named after Maria, the wife of Alexander II. It was renamed the **Kirov Theater,** after the prominent Communist leader under Stalin, in 1935. The gorgeous five-tiered theater is decorated with blue velvet chairs, gilded stucco, ceiling paintings and chandeliers; it seats 1,700.

Kirov Ballet Theater

In the 19th century, St Petersburg was the musical capital of Russia. At the Mariinsky Theater, premiers of opera and ballet were staged by Russia's most famous composers, dancers and singers. Under Petipa, Ivanov and Fokine, Russian ballet took on world-wide recognition. The Fyodor Chalyapin Memorial Room, named after the great singer, is open inside the Kirov during performances. The Kirovsky Theatre of Opera and Ballet continues to stage some of the world's finest ballets and operas; its companies tour many countries throughout the world. Performances are often sold out; check at the Intourist Desk at your hotel for tickets.

Opposite the Kirov stands the **Rimsky-Korsakov State Conservatory**, Russia's first advanced school of music. The founder of the Conservatory was the composer, Anton Rubenstein. Some of the graduates include Tchaikovsky, Prokofiev and Shostakovich. The Conservatory was given the name of Rimsky-Korsakov, who once managed the school, in 1944. On either side of the Conservatory stand the monuments to Mikhail Glinka and Rimsky-Korsakov. The Rimsky-Korsakov Museum is at 28 Zagorodny Prospekt. It is open from 11 am–5 pm, closed on Fridays and Saturdays. Further down Decembrists Prospekt, past the Kirov, is a Jewish synagogue.

A Simple Life

*E*ven at those hours when the gray Petersburg sky is completely overcast and the whole population of clerks have dined and eaten their fill, each as best he can, according to the salary he receives and his personal tastes; when they are all resting after the scratching of pens and bustle of the office, their own necessary work and other people's, and all the tasks that an overzealous man voluntarily sets himself even beyond what is necessary; when the clerks are hastening to devote what is left of their time to pleasure; some more enterprising are flying to the theater, others to the street to spend their leisure staring at women's hats, some to spend the evening paying compliments to some attractive girl, the star of a little official circle, while some—and this is the most frequent of all—go simply to a fellow clerk's apartment on the third or fourth story, two little rooms with a hall or a kitchen, with some pretensions to style, with a lamp or some such article that has cost many sacrifices of dinners and excursions—at the time when all the clerks are scattered about the apartments of their friends, playing a stormy game of whist, sipping tea out of glasses, eating cheap biscuits, sucking in smoke from long pipes, telling, as the cards are dealt, some scandal that has floated down from higher circles, a pleasure which the Russian can never by any possibility deny himself, or, when there is nothing better to talk about, repeating the everlasting anecdote of the commanding officer who was told that the tail had been cut off the horse on the Falconet monument—in short, even when everyone was eagerly seeking entertainment, Akaky Akakievich did not indulge in any amusement. No one could say that they had ever seen him at an evening party. After working to his heart's content, he would go to bed, smiling at the thought of the next day and wondering what God would send him to copy. So flowed on the peaceful life of a man who knew how to be content with his fate on a salary of four hundred roubles, and so perhaps it would have flowed on to extreme old age, had it not been for the various disasters strewn along the road of life.

Nikolai Gogol, 'The Overcoat',
translated by Constance Garnett

*

A walk down Glinka Prospekt leads to the Nikolsky Marine Cathedral (also functioning), built in 1753-62 by Chevakinsky in honor of St Nicholas, the protector of seamen. Naval officers once lived in the area, thus the full name of Nikolsky Morskoi (Marine). Standing at the intersection of the Griboyedov and Kryukov canals, the blue and white church combines the old Russian five-dome tradition with the baroque. A lovely carved wooden iconostasis is inside and a four-tiered belltower stands by itself in the gardens.

Up Glinka Prospekt in the opposite direction, the narrow *Potseluyev Most* (Bridge of Kisses) crosses the Moika River. To its right, the second building from the corner at no. 94 is the Palace of Culture of Educational Workers. This is an interesting spot because the last owner of the palace was the wealthy Count Yusupov, who was responsible for the assassination of Grigory Rasputin (the priest who exerted much influence in the court of Nicholas II) in the palace in 1916. Rasputin was first given poisoned cakes in the palace's basement, set up to look like a study. Nothing happened—the sugar in the cakes was thought to have neutralized the poison. Then the conspirators started shooting at Rasputin, and continued to do so as he ran from the house. Finally, they threw Rasputin's body through a hole in the ice of the Moika Canal. Later, after his body was found floating under the ice downstream, an autopsy showed that Rasputin had water in his lungs, proving he had still been alive after all the attempts to kill him. Yusupov later fled Russia.

Continuing along Glinka toward the Neva, a number of brick buildings are situated on a small triangular island. These were the storehouses for ship timber during the time of Peter the Great. Man-made canals created the small island known as Novaya Gollandiya (New Holland). The New Admiralty Canal, dug in 1717, connected the island with the Admiralty. Trade Union Boulevard was laid partly along the route of the old Admiralty canal.

The last square before the Neva is known as Labor Square, formerly Annunciation Square. Between 1853 and 1861, a palace for the oldest son of Nicholas I was built by Stakenschneider near the square. In 1895, it was turned into the Xenia Institute for Noble Ladies, named after Xenia, the daughter of Alexander II. In 1919, it was again turned over to the Trade Union Regional Council and renamed the **Palace of Labor**. At no. 44 Red Fleet Embankment is the State **Museum of the History of Leningrad** (closed on Wednesdays) in the former Rumyantsev Mansion.

Moscow Avenue

Moskovsky Prospekt runs for nearly 10 miles (16 kilometers) in a straight line from **Ploshchad Mira** (Peace Square) to the airport. The avenue follows the line known as the Pulkovo Meridian (zero on old Russian maps) that led to the Pulkovo Astronomical Observatory. The square was known, in Czarist times, as *Sennaya Ploshchad*, a place used for public punishment of serfs. Stagecoaches also left for Moscow from here. The area was the residence of many of Dostoevsky's characters— *Crime and Punishment's* Yeketerina Marmeladova, whose husband was killed, forced her children to perform for money near the canal. On **Grazhdanskaya Ulitsa** (Citizen's Prospekt) is the Raskolnikov House, from whose basement Raskolnikov stole the murder axe. "The houses of the murderer and his victim stood 730 paces apart". Raskolnikov knelt on the square hoping to repent for his crime.

A little past the Fontanka River is the **Moscow Triumphal Gate**, built in 1834-38 by Vassily Stasov to commemorate the Russian victories during the Russo-Turkish War of 1828-29. It was the largest cast-iron structure in the world in the mid-19th century. The gate is decorated with the Winged Victory, Glory, and Plenty and once marked the end of the city, where a road toll was collected. The closest Metro stop is Moskovskiye Vorota.

South of the gate, past the Kirov Elektrosila Factory, is the 170-acre (69 hectares) Moscow Victory Park, through which runs the Alley of Heroes. The park was laid out by tens of thousands of Leningraders after WW II in 1945. The Lenin Sports and Concert complex, seating 25,000, is located in the park. The closest Metro stop is Park Pobedy.

Farther along the prospekt on the left side is the Gothic red-white Chesma Palace and Church. Catherine the Great commissioned Felten to build it, so she could have a rest stop on the way to her country residences. It was named Chesma in 1770 after the Russian victory of the Turkish fleet at Chesma Bay. The Chesma Museum houses displays on the naval battle at Chesma. It is open 10 am– 5 pm, closed on Mondays and Tuesdays.

Next comes Moscow Square, whose whole eastern side is lined by the House of Soviets, with a Statue of Lenin at the center. Not far away is *Ploshchad Pobedy* (Victory Square). The **Monument to the Heroes of the Defense of Leningrad** (unveiled on May 9, 1975, 30 years after the seige) is the Square's focal point. The sculptured group, called The

Victors, look out to where the front once ran. Pink granite steps lead down to an obelisk that stands inside a circle symbolizing the breaking of the Blockade ring. An Eternal Flame is lit at the base. The ground floor of the base serves as a **Museum for the Seige of Leningrad**, open 10 am–6 pm, closed on Wednesdays. Closest Metro stop is Moskovskaya.

The Green Belt of Glory is a memorial complex that stretches 145 miles (230 kilometers) along the front line of 1941-44. Not far from the Baltic railway station, at Metro stop Narvskaya, is Strike Square with the **Narva Triumphal Gate** marking the victorious outcome of the War of 1812. Troups returning to St Petersburg after the war passed through the gate.

Piskarovskoye Memorial Cemetery lies to the south of Leningrad; open 10 am–6 pm daily. Here are the common graves, marked only by year of burial from 1941-44, of over a half million Leningraders who died during the 900-day seige. The Leningrad poet, Vera Inber, wrote: "Oh, this great city! How they tortured it—from earth and sky with freezing cold, with fire, and with starvation". The central path of the cemetery leads to the **Statue of the Mother Country**, holding a wreath of oak leaves, the symbol of eternal glory. Two museum pavilions are on either side of the entrance, where one realizes the horrors that faced the citizens of this city. Black and white photographs document the three-year blockade. The cemetery register is open at a page with the entries: "February, 1942: 18th—3,241 bodies; 19th—5,569; 20th—10,043". Another display shows a picture of 11-year-old Tanya Sevicheya and pages from her diary, "Granny died today. Mama died today. The Savichevs have died. Everybody died. Only Tanya is alive". Tanya later died after she was evacuated from the city. Behind the statue, carved on the memorial's walls are words by the Leningrad poet, Olga Bergholts:

"Here lie the people of Leningrad,
Here are the citizens—men, women and children...
They gave their lives
Defending you, Leningrad,
Cradle of Revolution.
We cannot number all their noble names here,
So many lie beneath the eternal granite,
But of those honored by this stone,
Let no one forget
Let nothing be forgotten".

Vicinity of Leningrad

If you have time, go on a few excursions outside Leningrad. Daytrips to Peter the Great's Summer Palace on the Gulf of Finland or to the towns of Pushkin and Pavlovsk are recommended!

Petrokrepost

Peter's Fortress, Petrokrepost, on a small island near the southwestern shore of Lake Ladoga, was founded by Slavs in 1323 to protect the trade waterways linking Novgorod with the Baltic. At that time, the small outpost was known as Oreshek (Nut). When Peter the Great captured the tiny fortress in 1702 from the Swedes (they took control of the lands in the 17th century), he renamed it Schlüsselburg, the Key Fortress. The town of Schlüsselburg sprang up along the left bank of the Neva, where it flows out of the lake. After the Northern War ended in 1721, Peter converted the fortress into a prison. He had his sister, Maria, and first wife, Evdokiya Lopukhina, imprisoned here; many other Russian revolutionaries suffered similar fates. On May 8, 1887, Lenin's brother, Alexander Ulyanov, along with four others who attempted to assassinate Czar Alexander III, were hung in the prison yard. The German name of Schlüsselburg was changed to Petrokrepost in 1944 during World War II. If you would like to visit Petrokrepost, and it is not included in your tour, check at your hotel's travel desk; Intourist offers daily bus excursions to the fortress or you can reach it by car.

Kronstadt

When Peter the Great began to build St Petersburg in 1703, the Northern War (1700-1721) with the Swedes was in its early stages. In order to protect the sea approaches to his new city, Peter built the Kronstadt Fortress, which also contained his shipyards, on the small island of Kotlin in the Gulf of Finland in 1704. The many monuments on the island are linked to the history of the Russian fleet. Intourist offers bus excurions to Kronstadt from Leningrad. A ferry also leaves from the town of Lomonosov. On the way, take notice of the 18-mile-long (29 kilometers) "barrier" that is being built across a section of the Gulf of Finland to control the frequent floods (over 300 in Leningrad's history). Tidal waves get swept inland during severe storms. In 1824, the water level rose 12 feet, killing 569 people.

Petrodvorets

While Peter the Great was supervising the building of the Kronstadt fortress, he stayed in a small lodge on the southern shore of the Gulf of Finland. After Russia defeated the Swedes in the Battle of Poltava in 1709, Peter decided to build his summer residence, Peterhof, so that it not only commemorated the victory over Sweden (and of gaining access to the Baltic), but also the might of the Russian empire. Peterhof was designed to resemble the French Palace of Versailles.

Architects were summoned from around the world: Rastrelli, Le Blond, Braunstein, Michetti and the Russian, Zemtsov. Over 4,000 peasants and soldiers were brought in to dig the canals, gardens and parks in the marshy area. Soil, building materials and tens of thousands of trees were brought in by barge. Peter helped to draft the layout of all the gardens and fountains. The fountains were built by Vasily Tuvolkov, Russia's first hydraulics engineer. Over 12 miles (20 kilometers) of canals were constructed in a way so that 30,000 liters (7,500 gallons) of water flowed under its own pressure (without the aid of a single pump) to 144 fountains.

The great **Cascade Fountain** in front of the palace has 17 waterfalls, 142 water jets, 66 fountains (including the two cup fountains on either side), 29 bas reliefs, and 39 gilded statues, including the famous Samson—the Russians won the Battle of Poltava on St Samson's Day. The five-ton Samson, surrounded by eight dolphins, is wrestling open the jaws of a lion, from which a jet of water shoots over 20 meters into the air.

Approaching the back of the palace from Red Avenue, the first fountain is known as the **Mezheumny**, with a dragon in the center pool. The **Neptune Fountain** was brought to Russia from Nuremberg, Germany. The **Oak Fountain** and Square Ponds are right by the walls of the palace in the Upper Park.

The northeast path leading to **Alexander Park** takes you by the Gothic Court chapel (with 43 saints along the outer walls), the **Cottage** (built in 1829 by Adam Menelaws, who designed it to resemble an aristocratic Englishman's cottage), and the **Farm**. This was also built by Menelaws as a storagehouse, but was later turned into a small summer palace by Alexander II. Following the path back around to the palace, you will come upon the **Conservatory**, used as a greenhouse. Nearby is

the **Triton Fountain**, which shows Neptune's son wrestling with a sea monster. **Chess Hill**, with a black and white checkerboard design, contains some of the best waterfalls, cascading over bronzed dragons. The two **Roman Fountains** (modeled after those at the Cathedral of St Peter in Rome) stand at the bottom of the hill and were designed by Karl Blank.

Following the path around to the right of the palace brings you to the **Pyramid Fountain**. Peter the Great designed this water pyramid, made up of seven tiers and 505 jets. A circular seat is positioned under the **Little Umbrella Fountain**. If you are tempted to have a short rest on the bench under the umbrella, be ready to scramble—as 164 jets spray out water as soon as anyone sits down! As you scamper away, you will approach the **Little Oak Fountain**, which has dozens of hidden jets (as do the artificial tulips) that spray as any weight approaches the oak tree. When you run off to the nearby bench to catch your breath, you will now get completely drenched from 41 more jets! Beware of the three fir trees too!

Approaching Monplaisir, the sun fountain shoots out from a rectangular pond as 16 golden dolphins swim around shiny disks. Jets of water sprinkle out from the center column, creating the golden rays of the sun. The **Adam and Eve fountains** (the statues were done by the Venetian sculpturer Bonazza) stand on either side of the path leading to the Gulf from the Palace.

While the Grand Palace was under construction, Peter designed and lived in the smaller Dutch-style villa that he called **Monplaisir** (My Pleasure), right on the Gulf of Finland. Even after the larger palace was completed, Peter preferred to stay here while he visited Peterhof. The two-story house, by the water on the other side of the palace, was known as the **Chateau de Marly**, built in 1714 in Louis XIV style—Peter visited a French king's hunting lodge in Marly. Behind it flows the **Golden Hill Cascade**. The other quaint two-story structure is known as the **Hermitage Pavilion**. It was built by Johann Friedrich Braunstein. The retreat was surrounded by a moat and had a drawbridge that could be raised to further isolate the guests. The first floor consisted of one room with a large dining room table that could be lifted from or lowered to servants on the ground floor; the guests placed a note on the table, rang a bell, and the table would shortly reappear with the orders. The **Lion Cascade Fountains** stand in front of the Hermitage.

The original palace was built between 1714 and 1724, designed in the baroque and classical styles. It stands on a hill in the center of the Peterhof complex and overlooks the parks and gardens. Rastrelli enlarged it (1747-54) for Empress Elizabeth. After Peter's death, the palace passed on to subsequent czars. It was declared a museum after the revolution. During World War II, the name Peterhof was changed to *Petrodvorets*, Peter's Palace. The palace is three stories high and attached by wings that contain the galleries. The central part contains the Exhibition Rooms, Peter the Great's Oak Study and the Royal Bedchamber. The rooms themselves have magnificent parquet floors, gilded ceilings, crystal chandeliers, and are filled with exquisite *objets d' art* from around the world. The **Crimson Room** has furniture by Chippendale; the walls of the oak study are covered by the portraits of the Empress Elizabeth, Catherine the Great and Alexander I; the **Partridge Chamber**, so named for the silk ornamental partridges that covered the walls, is filled with French silk-upholstered furniture, porcelain and clocks.

The **Portrait Gallery**, in the central hall of the palace, is filled with portraits by such painters as Pietro Rotari (the whole collection was acquired by Catherine the Great) and serves as an interesting catalog of the costumes of the period. The **White Dining Hall**, used for State dinners, is decorated in the classical style with white molded figures on the walls and a beautiful crystal and amethyst chandelier. The table is ceremoniously laid out for 30 people with 196 pieces of English porcelain. Rastrelli built the adjacent **Throne Room** for official receptions. A portrait of Catherine the Great on horseback hangs over Peter's first throne.

The **Chesma Room** commemorated the battles between the Russian and Turkish fleets in Chesma Bay in the Aegean Sea. The German artist, Hackert, was commissioned to paint the pictures in the room honoring the victories. Count Orlov (a squadron commander at Chesma) checked the artist's sketches and was dissatisfied with one that depicted an exploding ship. Hackert mentioned that he had never seen one. Orlov ordered a 60-cannon Russian frigate, anchored off the coast of Italy, to be packed with gunpowder. Hackert had to journey to Italy to see the ship exploding. The rest of the palace is joined by numerous galleries and studies. At the east end is a Rastrelli rococo chapel with five gilded cupolas.

Hitler invaded Russia on June 22, 1941. When, on September 23, 1941, the Nazis reached Peterhof, many of the art pieces and statues had still

not been evacuated. The Germany Army spent 900 days here and destroyed the complex. Monplaisir was an artillery site, used to shell Leningrad. The Germans cut down 15,000 trees for firewood, used tapestries in the trenches, plundered over 34,000 works of art, and made off with priceless objects, including the Samson statue, which were never recovered. After the war, massive restoration work began, and on June 17, 1945, the fountains flowed once again. The head of the Hermitage, Joseph Orbelli, who lived in the Hermitage during the seige, remarked: "Even during our worst suffering, we knew that the day would come when once again the beautiful fountains of Petrodvorets would begin to spray and the statues of the park flash their golden gleam in the sunlight". There are black-and-white photographs on display in the Exhibition Room that show the extensive damage to the palace.

Leningrad poet, Olga Bergholts, after visiting Peterhof after the siege, wrote:

"Again from the black dust, from the place
of death and ashes, will arise the garden as before.
So it will be. I firmly believe in miracles.
You gave me that belief, my Leningrad" .

Getting There

The Upper and Lower parks and gardens cover about 300 acres (121 hectares), stretching around the palace to the Gulf of Finland. When it is warm and clear, it is wonderful to have a picnic (bring food) on the grounds or beach, stroll in the gardens and spend the entire day. Daily tour buses run (20 miles/32 kilometers) from Leningrad, and Intourist offers group excursions (check at the hotel service desk). An electric train also leaves from the Baltic station to the stop, Novy Peterhof (35 minutes).

A much more interesting way to get there is by hydrofoil, known as the **Rocket.** This jets across the Gulf of Finland to the palace grounds in about 30 minutes. Catch one at the dock right across from the Hermitage (also opposite Decembrists' Square)—the hydrofoils run about every 20 minutes (May through September) and cost less than two rubles each way. (Intourist also offers daily group excursions. Inquire at your hotel.) Get there early to buy the ticket, since there tend to be long lines.

Besides your boat ticket, you will also be issued a separate ticket to get into the palace grounds. Do not lose it—you need to show it when you enter the complex from the dock. Typical of the Russian love of paper, this ticket will not admit you into the palace itself! Buy *this* ticket (for a few *kopeks*) at the small kiosk at the end of the dock. The palace is a good 10-minute walk from the docks; if you do not have an entrance ticket, you must walk all the way back!

Also, it is a good idea to buy your return ticket as soon as you arrive at Petrodvorets. If you wait til the last minute on a crowded day, all tickets for the time you want to return may be sold out. The return-ticket kiosks are to your left across the bridge as you get off the dock. A boat number will be stamped on the back of your ticket. When on the dock, look for your boat no. posted on signs.

The palace is open daily from 11 am–6 pm (and the fountains operate from May to September). The Grand Palace is closed on Monday and the last Tuesday of each month. Monplasir and the Hermitage are closed on Wednesday and the last Thursday of each month. The Chateau de Marly is closed on Tuesday and the last Wednesday of each month. In June, during the White Nights, many festivals are held the palace grounds.

Lomonosov

Once known as **Oranienbaum**, Lomonosov is situated only six miles (10 kilometers) west of Petrodvorets. Peter the Great gave the lands to his close friend, Prince Alexander Menschikov, to develop. Menschikov was the first governor-general of St Petersburg and supervised the building of the nearby Kronstadt Fortress. He turned the estate into his summer residence. Since he planted orange trees in the lower parks and grew them in hothouses, Menschikov named his residence *Oranienbaum*, German for "orange trees". The estate served as the country residence for later czars. Peter III and Catherine the Great expanded the buildings and grounds in the style of the times. In 1948, the name was changed to Lomonosov after the great Russian scientist, who had a glasswork factory nearby.

The estate escaped major shelling during the war and is beautifully preserved. The two-story Grand Palace (1725, by architects Fontane and Shedel) stands atop a hill overlooking parks and gardens that were originally designed by Antonio Rinaldi, who also built the two pleasure pavilions, the **Chinese Palace** and **Katalnaya Gorka**, (Sliding Hill). Visitors could glide on sleds along a wooden path from the third story of the pavilion and, building up speed, ride down throughout the lower parks.

Oranienbaum became the center of masqued balls and parties that entertained Russian royalty and foreign diplomats. Pushkin, Nekrasov, Dumas, Turgenev, Tolstoy, Mussorgsky and Repin were frequent guests. The estate is now a museum (buildings closed on Tuesday) and can be reached by bus, car, by a train which leaves from Leningrad's Baltic Station, or by ferry from Kronstadt.

Pushkin

The town of Pushkin, 15.5 miles (25 kilometers) south of Leningrad, was formerly known as **Czarskoye Selo**, the Czar's Village. After the Revolution, the named was changed to **Detskoye Selo** (Children's Village), and many of the town's buildings were made into schools. The poet, Pushkin, studied at the Lyceum (1811-17). In 1937, to commemorate the 100-year anniversary of Pushkin's death, the town was renamed Pushkin.

The Moskovsky Prospekt was built in the early 18th century to connect the Royal Residence to St Petersburg. The road continued all the way to Moscow. On the way to Pushkin, the road passes through Pulkovo Heights, where the famed **Pulkovo Observatory** is situated. It was badly damaged during the war; now restored, Pulkovo is one of the main observatories in the country. After crossing the Kuzminka River, you come to the Egyptian Entrance Gates (1830) of the city. The gates were designed by the British architect, Adam Menelaws, who incorporated motifs from the Egyptian temples at Karnak. To the left of the gate is a statue of Alexander Pushkin.

Peter the Great won the region between the Neva and the Gulf of Finland during the Northern War, including the area of the town. He gave these lands to Prince Menschikov, but later took them back and presented all to his wife, Catherine II. She built terraced parks and gardens and the **Yekaterininsky Dvorets**, Catherine's Palace. In 1752, the Empress Elizabeth commissioned Rastrelli to renovate the palace. The beautiful baroque building stretches 900 feet (300 meters) and is decorated with statues, columns and gold ornaments.

Catherine the Great built additions to the palace. During her reign, many renowned architects, such as Cameron, Rinaldi and Quarenghi, worked in the neo-classical style on the palace. Many exhibition halls, Cameron's **Green Dining Room** and **Chinese Blue Room** are breathtaking. The walls of the **Blue Room** are decorated with Chinese blue silk and the Empress Elizabeth is portrayed as Flora, Goddess of Flowers.

Catherine the Great

Peter the Great propelled Russia into the beginning of the 18th century. Catherine II completed it by decorating his creation in European pomp and principle. Catherine was a German princess who was given in marriage to Peter III, the homely grandson of Peter the Great. When her husband died of mysterious circumstances in 1762, Catherine became the first foreigner ever to sit upon the Russian throne. Catherine was clever and adventurous and had fallen (instead of with her husband) deeply in love with her new homeland. She immersed herself in the problems of politics and agriculture and worked toward basing the government on philosophic principles rather than on religious doctrines or hereditary rights. Because of her European roots, Catherine held a fascination for France and avidly worked to link French culture with that of her adopted nation. She read Voltaire, Montesquieu and Rousseau and sent emissaries to study in foreign lands; she also began the education of noblewomen. The Russian aristocracy soon incorporated French culture into their daily lives, giving the noblemen a common identity. The French language also set them apart from the Russian peasantry.

Catherine described her reign as the "thornless rose that never stings". Along with autocratic power, she ruled with virtue, justice and reason. By the publication of books and newspapers, and instruction by Western-trained tutors, education spread throughout the provinces, where before much of the learning originated from the Church. This allowed Russian culture to cut loose from its religious roots. Paper money was introduced, along with vaccinations; the day of Catherine's smallpox vaccination became a national feast day.

Scientific expeditions were sent to far eastern lands and hundreds of new cities were built in Russia's newly conquered territories. Along the coast of the Black Sea, the cities of Odessa, Azov and Sevastopol were constructed on the sites of old Greek settlements. With the formation of the Academy of Sciences, Russia now contributed to the Renaissance Age and would never again stand in the shadows. One of the most important figures of the time, Mikhail Lomonosov, scientist, poet and historian, later helped to establish Moscow University.

Catherine spared no expense to redecorate St Petersburg in the classical designs of the time. Wanting a home for the art that she began collecting from abroad, Catherine built the Hermitage. It was connected to her private apartments and also served as a conference chamber and theater. Besides the exquisite treasures kept within, the Hermitage itself was constructed of jasper, malachite, marble and gold. The Empress also had an extravagant reputation which filtered into her love life as well; she had 21 known lovers.

Unfortunately it became increasingly difficult for Catherine to maintain her autocratic rule while at the same time implement large-scale reform. Her sweeping plans for change planted the seeds for much more of a blossoming than she bargained for. The education of the aristocracy created a greater schism between them and the working class and her reforms further worsened the conditions of the peasantry. As the city took the center of culture away from the Church, more and more Old Believers were left disillusioned with her rule. Catherine tore down monasteries and torched the old symbols of Moscovy. In an Age of Reason, she had a deep suspicion of anything mystical.

Huge sums of money were also spent on constructing elaborate palaces for her favorite relations and advisors. One of these was Prince Grigory Potemkin, her foreign minister, commander-in-chief and greatest love for almost two decades. It was he who organized a trip for Catherine down the Dnieper River to view the newly accessed Crimean territories. The prince had painted façades constructed along the route to camouflage the degree of poverty of the peasants. These "Potemkin Villages" were also to give the appearance of real towns in the other-wise uninhabited areas. Finally in 1773, Pugachev, a Don Cossack, led a rebellion of impoverished Cossacks, peasants and Old Believers against the throne and serfdom. Pugachev was captured and sentenced to decapitation, but ended up exiled in Siberia.

It was not only the peasantry and the Church that felt alientated. The aristocracy too grew dissatisfied with the new European truths and philosophies. Those who yearned for more considered themselves a new class, the intelligentsia. Searching for their own identity amidst a surge of French principles, the intelligentsia pro-ceeded not only to understand Voltaire's logic but to incorporate the heart and the spirit as well.

By grasping the ideals of a foreign Enlightenment, Catherine II unknowingly gave birth to Russia's own. The catalyst of change, along with teaching people to think for themselves, brought despotism into deeper disfavor and paved the road to revolution. After the fall of the Bastille, Catherine turned her back on France. In a panic, she tried to dispose of all that she had helped create. Censorship was imposed throughout Russia, and Catherine attempted to slam shut the window to the West less than a century after Peter had opened it. But from this period of discontent and new search for meaning, Russia would give birth to some of the greatest writers and thinkers of all time. The West would be captivated by the works of Pushkin, Dostoevsky and Tolstoy, and Lenin would later lead Russia out of five centuries of autocratic rule. Peter the Great had built the wheels and Catherine set them in motion; there was to be no turning back.

*The interior splendor of
Catherine the Great's Palace*

The Old Guard

*A*n old man of eighty-four attracted my attention in the Mikhailovsky gardens. He brandished a sabre-shaped walking-stick as he strode down the paths, his war medals dangled in ranks at his chest, and his features showed bellicose above a mist of white beard. He looked like God the Father peering over a cloud.

'I'm an Old Bolshevik,' he announced to me. 'One of the original Revolutionaries!'

A ghost from the twenties, he still exulted in the people's common ownership. He patted the tree trunks possessively as he marched by and frequently said 'This is my tree, and this is my tree.'

In 1907 he had become a revolutionary, and had been sent in chains to Siberia. But a fellow-prisoner, he said, had concealed a file in the lapel of his coat, and together they had cut through their manacles and fled back to Leningrad. Those were the days when Siberian exiles and prisoners—Trotsky, Stalin and Bakunin among them—escaped from Siberia with laughable ease and slipped over frontiers with the freedom of stray cats.

Then the old man had joined the Revolution and fought for three years against the Whites. He settled into a military stride as he spoke of it, and thrust out his beard like a torpedo, while all the time his gaze flashed and fulminated over the gardens. 'Get off the grass, comrade!' he bellowed. A young mother, seated on the sward beside her pram, looked up in bewilderment. 'Get off our motherland's grass!'

He embodied the intrusive precepts of early Communism, whose zealots were encouraged to scrutinize, shrive and denounce each other. He was the self-proclaimed guardian and persecutor of all about him, and he entered the 1980s with the anachronism of a mastodon. Farther on a girl was leaning in the fork of one of his precious trees. 'Keep away from there!' he roared. 'Can't you see you're stopping it grow? Get off!' She gaped at him, said nothing, did not move. He marched on unperturbed. He even anathematized a mousing cat. 'What are you looking for, comrade? Leave nature alone!' He did not seem to mind or notice that nobody obeyed him.

We rested under a clump of acacias. 'When I was a boy,' he said, 'I saw these trees planted.' He pointed to the largest of them, which bifurcated into a gnarled arm. 'That tree was no taller than a little lamp-post then. The garden was private, of course, but as a boy I often squeezed in over the railings. The tsar and tsaritsa used to walk here in the summer.' His voice dwindled from an alsatian growl to purring reminiscence. 'Once, while I was hiding in the shrubs, I saw them myself... What were they like? It's hard to recall exactly. But she was a beautiful woman, I remember. She had her hand on his arm. And he seemed very large and handsome, and ...' But he never finished. The lurking commissar in him erupted again. 'What are you doing, comrade?' Beneath us, a man was raking weeds out of an ornamental pond. 'How can you weed a lake?'

The gardener looked up stoically. 'I'm at work.'

Work. The magic syllable.

Immediately, as if some benedictory hand had passed its grace across the old man's brow, his expression changed to a look of benign redress. 'Fine', he murmured, 'work.' For him the word had the potency of 'revolution' or 'collective'. The mousing cat, too, had been at work, I thought, but had been unable to voice this watchword.

Before we parted he said: 'I'll give you my address. It's just a postal address, not the real one. That's secret. You see,' he repeated, 'I'm one of the Old Bolsheviks.'

I wondered then if he were not deranged. He scribbled out his address on the back of a newspaper, in enormous handwriting. It was only as he was leaving me that I realized from his age that the history he had given me was nonsense. The tsars did not send lone boys of eleven to Siberia.

'How old did you say you were?' I asked. For he looked timeless.

'I know what you're thinking,' he answered. His eyes twinkled at me collusively. 'You Estonians, you're a clever lot. You're thinking that I can't have been sent to Siberia aged eleven. But actually I'm ninety-four...'— and he strode away through the trees.

Colin Thubron, Among the Russians

The white marble staircase leading into the palace was built in 1860 by Monighetti. On the inside walking tour, you pass through Rastrelli's **Cavalier Dining Room** and **Great Hall**. Peter the Great traded 248 personal guards with a Prussian king in exchange for panels of amber. Rastrelli built the **Amber Room** with these panels in 1755. During WW II, the Nazis made off with the panels, which were never found. The **Picture Hall** stretches the entire width of the building; of the 130 French, Flemish and Italian canvasses that were here before the war, 117 were evacuated and can be seen today. The palace chapel was begun by Rastrelli and completed by Stasov. The northeast section of the palace, in the chapel wing, contains the **Pushkin Museum**, made up of 27 halls, displaying his personal belongings and manuscripts.

The Lyceum is linked to the Palace by an archway. It was originally built by Catherine the Great as the school for her grandsons and was expanded in 1811 for the children of the aristocracy. The classrooms were on the second floor and the dormitory on the third. The Lyceum's first open class consisted of 30 boys between 11 and 14. One of these students was Alexander Pushkin. The Lyceum is now a museum and the classrooms and laboratories are kept as they were during Pushkin's time. A room in the dormitory reads, "Door no. 14 Alexander Pushkin". Pushkin read aloud his poem "Recollections of Czarskoye Selo" on June 9, 1817, in the school's Assembly hall. The statue of Pushkin outside was sculpted by Robert Bach in 1900. The church (1734-47) next to the Lyceum is the oldest building in the town.

Catherine's parks consisted of three types: the French one was filled with statues and pavilions, the English had more trees and shrubs, and the Italian contained more sculpted gardens. The grounds stretch over 1,400 acres (567 hectares). Rastrelli built the Orlov column in the middle of the lake as a monument to the victory at the Battle of Chesma. The Hermitage structure was built between 1744 and 1756 to entertain the guests. No servants were allowed on the second floor. The guests wrote requests on slates; the tables were lowered and raised with the appropriate drink and dishes, including some like elk lips and nightingale tongues! The adjacent fish canal provided seafood for the royal banquets. The upper bath house was used by the royal family and the lower by the visitors.

Other buildings on the estate include the Admiralty (with a boat collection), the Grotto (once decorated with over 250,000 shells), the Cameron Gallery, the Hanging Gardens, the Agate Rooms, the Granite

Terrace, Marble Bridge (made from Siberian marble), Turkish Baths (resembling a mosque) and the Milkilometersaid Fountain (built in 1816 by Sokolov from a fable by La Fontaine). Pushkin wrote a poem based on the fable about the sad girl who holds a piece of her milk jug that lies broken at her feet. The Alexander Palace was built by Catherine the Great (1792-96 by Quarenghi) for her grandson, the future Alexander I. Nicholas I lived here after the 1905 revolution in St Petersburg.

Many bus excursions run to Pushkin (check at Intourist). Another easy way to the town is by electric train from Leningrad's Vitebsky Station (from Pushkinskaya Metro to stop Detskoye Selo). From the station in Pushkin, grab a local bus or taxi to the palace. The palace is open 11 am–6 pm, closed on Tuesdays. The Lyceum is closed on Thursdays.

Pavlovsk

The gay court life of Czarskoye Selo scared away most of the wildlife. So the royal family went into the nearby area of **Pavlovskoye** (about two miles/four kilometers away) to hunt. Two wooden hunting lodges were known as "Krik" and "Krak". In 1777, Catherine the Great presented the villages, along with the serfs, to her son, Pavel (Paul), whose first son, Alexander, had just been born. The village was renamed Pavlovsk when Paul became czar. The Scottish architect, Cameron, began building the palace in the 1780s and Paul turned it into his official summer residence. Pavlovsk Park was created by Pietro Gonzaga (who lived here from 1803 to 1838) and covers over 3,750 acres (1,500 hectares), making it one of the largest landscaped parks in the world, with designs such as the Valley of the Ponds and the White Birchtree. Cameron also designed the Pavilion of Three Graces, the Temple of Friendship (1782) and the Apollo Colonnade (1783). Other structures include the Twelve Paths (and 12 bronze statues), Pavilion of the Monument to My Parents (of Paul I's wife), and the Mausoleum of Paul I (the murdered czar is buried in the Peter and Paul Fortress).

The architects, Cameron, Brenna, Rossi, Quarenghi and Voronikhin, all worked on the construction of the palace, with its 64 columns and yellow façade. The palace contains an Egyptian vestibule, Italian, French and Greek Halls, library, dressing room of Empress Maria Fyodorovna and Paul I, the throne room, orchestral chambers, billiard and ballrooms and picture galleries.

The palace and grounds were virtually destroyed during the war, but have been beautifully restored. Pavlovsk is 19 miles (30 kilometers) south of Leningrad. You can take a bus tour (check at Intourist) combining both Pushkin and Pavlovsk in the same day. You can also get there by electric train from Leningrad's Vitebsk station (Pushinskaya Metro stop). Drivers should leave the car by the wooden bridge and walk to the palace, open from 11 am–6 pm and closed on Thursdays and Fridays. It is an enjoyable excursion all season long. There is boating in the summer and skiing, ice skating and *troika* rides in the winter.

Gatchina

The village of **Gatchina**, 28 miles (45 kilometers) southwest of Leningrad, was first mentioned in 15th century chronicles. In the early 18th century, Peter the Great presented his sister, Natalia, with a farm in the area. Later, Catherine the Great gave the villages as a present to her lover Count Orlov; he had a castle built by Rinaldi in 1781. Paul I (Catherine's son) later took control of the lands and redesigned the palace into a medieval castle. Being a paranoid czar (he was later murdered), Paul had the architect Brenna build a moat with a drawbridge, sentry boxes, tollgates and a fortress around the castle. Gatchina Park surrounds White Lake.

Behind Long Island is Silver Lake, which never freezes over. The first Russian submarine was tested here in 1879. At the end of the lake there is a lovely little Temple to Venus on the Island of Love. The Castle and grounds, badly damaged during WW II, have not totally been restored. But it is a lovely place to walk around and here one can really take notice of the havoc caused by German shelling to Leningrad and the environs during World War II. The area can be reached as a bus tour or by car.

Razliv

Leningrad and its environs have over 300 places connected with the life of Lenin. To hide from the Provisional Government in 1917, Lenin came to the village of Razliv, 22 miles (35 kilometers) northwest of the city on the Karelian Isthmus near the former Finnish border. Agents were searching everywhere for him and advertised a reward of 200,000 rubles in gold. Shaving off his trademark beard and wearing a wig, he ventured out in the darkness of night from the Finland railroad station to the village, and stayed in a barn owned by the Yemelyanov family. A few days later Nikolai Yemelyanov rowed Lenin across Lake Razliv and built a hut out of hay for a more secretive shelter. A haystack and hut stand on the spot where Lenin lived. There are museums in the hut and barn   and a glass pavilion stands near the hut, exhibiting Lenin's personal belongings and documents. There are bus tours to Razliv (check at Intourist) and a tourist boat takes visitors across the lake. You can also get there by electric train (toward Sestroretsk) from the Finland railway station. Razliv is open from 10 am to 6 pm and closed on Wednesdays.

Repino

The road from Razliv along the Karelian Isthmus leads to Repino and the town of Sestroretsk about 20 miles (32 kilometers) northwest of Leningrad. Repino is a small town in the resort area once known as Kurnosovo. It now bears the name of the celebrated painter, Ilya Repin (1844-1930), who bought a cottage in the settlement in 1899 and made it his permanent residence. All his friends and students gathered there every Wednesday and Repin painted the rest of the week. Repin named his estate **The Penates**, after the Roman gods of home and well-being. Repin is buried on the grounds. The Penates burned down during WW II, but was totally reconstructed and is now a museum, displaying Repin's art and personal belongings. You can get there by tour bus (Intourist) or car, or by electric train from Finland station in the direction of Vyborg, stop is Repino. The estate is open from 10.30 am–5.30 pm and closed on Tuesdays.

Novgorod

If there is time for a few other off-the-beaten-track excursions, a visit to **Novgorod** and **Pskov** is highly recommended (especially if you do not plan to tour a few towns in the Golden Ring area). Novgorod is about a three-hour drive from Leningrad—which really gets you into the Russian countryside.

Novgorod is one of the oldest towns in all of Russia, founded almost 1,200 years ago. The first Varangian leader, Rurik, settled here. The northern Slavs named the town Novgorod, meaning "New Town" by the shores of Ilmen Lake. The town served as the main northern trade center between the Varangians and the Greeks. As it grew, it became known as Novgorod the Great. In the 12th century, there were over 200

From Cradle To Grave

Melissino and I were present at an extraordinary ceremony on the Day of the Epiphany, namely the blessing of the Neva, then covered with five feet of ice.

After the benediction of the waters children were baptised by being plunged into a large hole which had been made in the ice. On the day on which I was present, the priest happened to let one of the children slip through his hands.

'Drugoi!' *he cried.*

That is, 'Give me another'. But my surprise may be imagined when I saw that the father and mother of the child were in an ecstasy of joy; they were certain that the babe had been carried straight to heaven. Happy ignorance!

Giovanni Jacopo Casanova de Seingalt, Memoirs, *translated from the Italian by Arthur Machen*

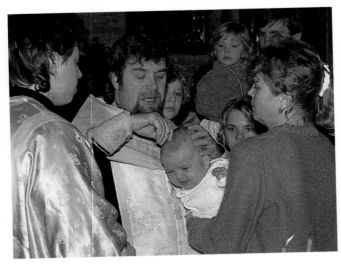

churches. It remained a center for trade and religion well into the 15th century, when it was annexed to Moscovy.

Novgorod is a good example of an old Russian town and a treasury of old Russian Church architecture (over 30 remain), paintings (icons, frescoes and mosaics) and history (birchbark manuscripts). The town is surrounded by a *kremlin*. Its most famous structure is the Cathedral of St Sophia (1045-50). Near the cathedral is a museum with 35 halls and 80,000 exhibitions. There is also the Open-air Museum of Old Wooden Architecture.

Pskov

Pskov is a few hours farther southwest of Novgorod. Another of Russia's most ancient towns, it was first mentioned in a chronicle in 903. Pskov began as a small outpost of Novgorod and later grew into a commercial center and developed its own school of icon painting. It is still filled with many beautiful churches and icons. Ivan the Terrible tried to annex Pskov, but the town resisted for many years before being subjugated. Rimsky-Korsakov later wrote an opera based on the uprisings called *The Maid of Pskov*. Nicholas II abdicated the throne while in his train at the Pskov station on March 15, 1917.

Accommodation

Intourist Hotels

Astoria, 39 Herzen Prospekt, located by St Isaacs Cathedral, tel. 219-1100; nearest Metro station Nevsky Prospekt. Recently renovated; one of Leningrad's oldest and most luxurious hotels. Rated Deluxe by Intourist.

Evropeiskaya, 1/7 Brodsky St., tel. 210-3295, nearest Metro station Nevsky Prospekt. Old, luxurious (recently renovated) and centrally located off Nevsky Prospekt. Rated Deluxe by Intourist.

Gaven, 88 Sredny Prospekt on Vasilyevsky Island, tel. 356-8504, nearest Metro station Primorskaya. Used mostly by visiting trade groups.

Leningrad, 5/2 Vyborgsky Embankment, tel. 542-9123, nearest Metro station Ploshchad Lenina. Modern Deluxe hotel. Located on north bank of Neva by Cruiser Aurora, but only a short hop into the city center. Ask for a view of the water.

Moskva, 2 Alexander Nevsky Square, tel. 274-9505/2051, nearest Metro Ploshchad Alexandra Nevskovo. Modern first-class hotel. Located by Alexander Nevsky Monastery, with easy access to the city center via Metro.

Olgino, Outside of town, tel. 238-3550. Modern standard hotel. Cheapest of the Intourist hotels, since it is located about 30 minutes by car or bus from the center of town. Has camping facilities in summer (must pre-book before arriving in country).

Olympia Hotel, Vasilyevsky Island, nearest Metro station Primorskaya. First-class accomodation aboard a Swedish ship. Excellent, but expensive; foreign currency restaurant. Ask for a view of the water.

Pribaltiiskaya, 14 Korablestroiteley Prospekt on Vasilyevsky Island, tel. 356-0263, nearest Metro station Primorskaya. Deluxe modern hotel (built by Swedes), with bowling alley and sauna. Ask for a view of the water. Restaurants Daugava and Neva on second floor. Cafeteria-type restaurant on first floor. Top floor foreign currency bar—the back serves hot meals for foreign currency. Each floor has a small café. Two large Beriozkas are outside and a smaller one inside on first floor.

Pulkovskaya, 1 Pobedy Square, tel. 264-5109, nearest Metro station Moskovskaya.

Food

All Intourist hotels have restaurants, café and bars. Swedish Table smorgasbords (*Svedski Stol*) are found at the Priba!tiiskaya, Evropeiskaya, Leningrad and Moskva hotels for breakfast, lunch and dinner. This is an excellent way to get an adequate and quick meal. Outside your hotel, many restaurants, cafés and co-operatives are located throughout the city.

Along Nevsky Prospekt

Druzhba, 15 Nevsky. The "Friendship" Café opens at 8 am and serves breakfast, lunch and dinner.

Minutka, 20 Nevsky. A cafeteria serving quick-snack soups, hot pies, desserts and coffee, cocoa and tea in a "minute".

Mercury, 22 Nevsky, tel. 311-7490. Serving pastries, ice-cream and drinks.

Ogonyok, 24 Nevsky. Specializes in ice-cream and drinks.

Kavkazsky, 25 Nevsky. One of the city's most popular restaurants of Caucasian dishes. Specials include the soup *kharcho*, chicken *tabak* and *chakhombili, chebureki*, small pies filled with lamb, rice and seasonings and *shashlik*.

"At Kazanskovo" Café, 26 Nevsky.

Nevsky Bar, 27 Nevsky. Foreign currency.

Literary Café, corner of Nevsky and the Moika Canal. Lovely restored 19th-century restaurant. (Here Pushkin met up with his second on the way to the tragic duel.) Good food, decorated with old pictures, and has music and literature recitals.

Sadko, corner of Nevsky and Brodsky next to the Evropeiskaya Hotel. Traditional Russian cooking, including *blini*, folk music, dancing and floor shows. The hard currency bar is open in the basement. Crowded with foreigners in summer, when advance reservations are needed.

40 Nevsky Bar and Café, 40 Nevsky. Foreign currency only.

Detsky. The "Children's" Café is at 42 Nevsky. The meals are intended for children; walls are decorated in fairy-tale motifs.

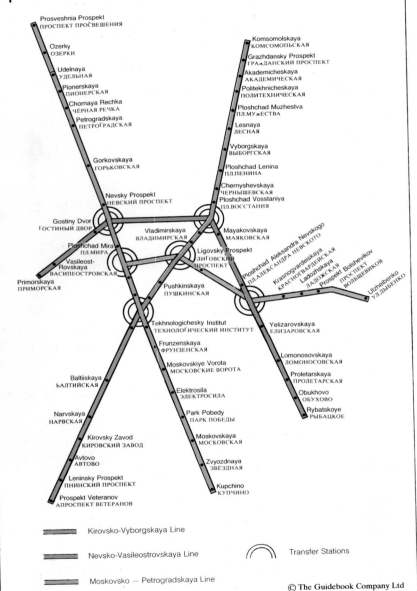

Leningrad Metro

Prosveshnia Prospekt
ПРОСПЕКТ ПРОСВЕЩЕНИЯ

Ozerky
ОЗЕРКИ

Udelnaya
УДЕЛЬНАЯ

Pionerskaya
ПИОНЕРСКАЯ

Chornaya Rechka
ЧЁРНАЯ РЕЧКА

Petrogradskaya
ПЕТРОГРАДСКАЯ

Gorkovskaya
ГОРЬКОВСКАЯ

Nevsky Prospekt
НЕВСКИЙ ПРОСПЕКТ

Gostiny Dvor
ГОСТИНЫЙ ДВОР

Ploshchad Mira
ПЛ.МИРА

Vasileost-
Rovskaya
ВАСИЛЕОСТРОВСКАЯ

Primorskaya
ПРИМОРСКАЯ

Vladimirskaya
ВЛАДИМИРСКАЯ

Ligovsky Prospekt
ЛИГОВСКИЙ
ПРОСПЕКТ

Pushkinskaya
ПУШКИНСКАЯ

Komsomolskaya
КОМСОМОЛЬСКАЯ

Grazhdansky Prospekt
ГРАЖДАНСКИЙ ПРОСПЕКТ

Akademicheskaya
АКАДЕМИЧЕСКАЯ

Politekhnicheskaya
ПОЛИТЕХНИЧЕСКАЯ

Ploshchad Muzhestva
ПЛ.МУЖЕСТВА

Lesnaya
ЛЕСНАЯ

Vyborgskaya
ВЫБОРГСКАЯ

Ploshchad Lenina
ПЛ.ПЕНИНА

Chernyshevskaya
ЧЕРНЫШЕВСКАЯ

Ploshchad Vosstaniya
ПЛ.ВОССТАНИЯ

Mayakovskaya
МАЯКОВСКАЯ

Ploshchad Aleksandra Nevskogo
ПЛ.АЛЕКСАНДРА НЕВСКОГО

Krasnogvardeiskaya
КРАСНОГВАРДЕЙСКАЯ

Ladozhskaya
ЛАДОЖСКАЯ

Prospekt Bolshevikov
ПРОСПЕКТ
БОЛЬШЕВИКОВ

Ulzheibenko
УЛ.ДЫБЕНКО

Tekhnologichesky Institut
ТЕХНОЛОГИЧЕСКИЙ ИНСТИТУТ

Frunzenskaya
ФРУНЗЕНСКАЯ

Moskovskiye Vorota
МОСКОВСКИЕ ВОРОТА

Baltiiskaya
ЬАЛТИЙСКАЯ

Narvskaya
НАРВСКАЯ

Kirovsky Zavod
КИРОВСКИЙ ЗАВОД

Avtovo
АВТОВО

Leninsky Prospekt
ПНИНСКИЙ ПРОСПЕКТ

Prospekt Veteranov
АПРОСПЕКТ ВЕТЕРАНОВ

Elektrosila
ЭЛЕКТРОСИЛА

Park Pobedy
ПАРК ПОБЕДЫ

Moskovskaya
МОСКОВСКАЯ

Zvyozdnaya
ЗВЁЗДНАЯ

Kupchino
КУПЧИНО

Yelizarovskaya
ЕЛИЗАРОВСКАЯ

Lomonosovskaya
ЛОМОНОСОВСКАЯ

Proletarskaya
ПРОЛЕТАРСКАЯ

Obukhovo
ОБУХОВО

Rybatskoye
РЫБАЦКОЕ

Kirovsko-Vyborgskaya Line

Nevsko-Vasileostrovskaya Line

Moskovsko — Petrogradskaya Line

Transfer Stations

© The Guidebook Company Ltd

Neva, 44-46 Nevsky. Leningrad's largest restaurant, seating over 1,000. Tasty dishes are the *shchi* soup, Neva-style fish and Sever ice-cream. The **Sever** (North) Café has good desserts; Leningrad's best cake shop.

Avtomat, A self-service cafeteria at 45 Nevsky.

Moskva, 49 Nevsky. Russian cuisine with good Moscow-style stuffed meats and pancakes.

Aurora, 60 Nevsky. Milk and cheese dishes.

Lancômb, 64 Nevsky.

Blinnaya, 74 Nevsky. A cellar café offering Russian pancakes with a choice of fillings that include red and black caviar, sour cream and fruit.

Leningrad, 96 Nevsky. The Russian idea of a 'low-cal' cafeteria.

Universal, 106 Nevsky.

Sadovaya (Garden) Prospekt

Metropole, 22 Garden Prospekt The oldest restaurant in the city is well known for the meat and fish dishes, and desserts. Next door is a shop that sells take-out food.

Lakomka, next to the Metropole. Serves a delicious variety of pastries, pies and cakes.

Baku, on Garden Street between Nevsky and Rakov streets. A popular restaurant with Azerbaijani and Caucasian cuisine. Bands, music and dancing in evenings. Reservations are usually needed.

Petrogradskaya Side

Kronwerk. A three-masted ship docked next to Peter and Paul Fortress in the Kronwerk Strait. Serves meals and drinks.

Austeria. Inside Peter and Paul Fortress near Peter's Gate. It offers dishes that were popular in the days of Peter the Great.

State of Siege

What an incredible thing is this feeling of hunger. One can get used to it as to a chronic headache. For two successive days I have been waiting with blind resignation for one glutinous piece of bread, without experiencing acute hunger. That means the disease (ie hunger) has gone over from the acute stage to the chronic.

It's dark. I couldn't stop myself from getting out that precious candle-end, hidden away in case of dire emergency. The darkness is terribly oppressive. Mila's dozing on the sofa. She is smiling in her sleep, she must be dreaming of a sandwich with smoked sausage or of thick barley soup. Every night she has appetising dreams, which is why waking up is especially tormenting for her.

The entire flat is appallingly cold, everything is frozen, stepping out into the corridor involves putting on one's coat, galoshes and hat. The bleakness of desolation everywhere. The water supply is non-existent, we have to fetch water from more than three kilometres away. The sewage system is a thing of the distant past—the yard is full of muck. This is like some other city, not Leningrad, always so proud of its European, dandyish appearance. To see it now is like meeting a man you have become accustomed to seeing dressed in a magnificent, thick woolen overcoat, sporting clean gloves, a fresh collar, and good American boots. And here you suddenly meet that same man completely transformed—clothed in tatters, filthy, unshaven, with foul-smelling breath and a dirty neck, with rags on his feet instead of boots.

Yesterday's Leningradskaya Pravda *published an article by the chairman of the Leningrad Soviet, comrade Popkov, entitled 'On the Leningrad Food Situation'. After calling on all citizens to summon their courage and patience, comrade Popkov goes on to speak of the very real problems of theft and abuse in Leningrad's food distribution network.*

My candle-end has almost burnt down. Soon darkness will descend upon me—until morning...

17th January. *Old age. Old age is the fatigue of well-worn components that are involved in the working of a human body, an exhaustion of man's inner resources. Your blood no longer keeps you warm, your legs refuse to obey you, your back grows stiff, your brain grows feeble, your memory fades. The pace of old age is as unhurried as the slow combustion of the almost burnt-out logs in a stove: the flames die away, lose their colour, one log disintegrates into golden embers, then another—and now the last flickering blue flames are fading—it will soon be time to shut off the flue.*

We are, all of us, old people now. Regardless of our age. The pace of old age now governs our bodies and our feelings... Yesterday at the market I saw a little girl of about nine, wearing enormous felt boots which were full of holes. She was bartering a chunk of dubious-looking brawn— probably made from dog meat—for 100 grammes of bread. Her eyes, hardly visible beneath a pair of heavy lids, looked terribly tired, her back was bent, her gait slow and shuffling, her face puckered and the corners of her mouth turned down. It was the face of an old woman. Can this ever be forgotten or forgiven?

23rd January, 11 a.m. *Slowly, laboriously, like emaciated people toiling up a hill, the days drag by. Monotonous, unhealthy, withdrawn days in a now silent city. Leningrad's nerve centres, which have until recently kept the life of the city going, fed it vital impulses—the power stations— have ceased to function. And all the nerve fibres extending over the city lie dormant, inactive. There is no light, no trams or trolley-buses are running, the factories, cinemas, theatres have all stopped working. It is pitch black in the empty shops, chemists', canteens—their windows having been boarded up since autumn (as protection from shell fragments). Only the feeble, consumptive flame of a wick-lamp flickers on every counter... Thickly coated in snow, the tram, trolley-bus and radio cables hang listlessly above the streets. They stretch overhead like an endless white net, and there is nothing to make them shed their thick snow cover.*

The great city's nervous system has ceased its function. But we know that this is not death, but only a lethargic sleep. The time will come when the sleeping giant will stir, and then rouse himself...

Alexander Dymov, winter of 1942, *translated by Hilda Perham*

Primorsky, 32 Bolshoi Prospekt.

Volshebny Krai, 15/3 Bolshoi Prospekt, tel. 233-3253. Hot dishes and non-alcoholic drinks.

Vasilyevsky Island
Fregat, 39/14 Bolshoi Prospekt. Offers traditional Russian dishes— many were popular in the time of Peter the Great.

Olympia. Inside a Swedish ship docked on the Gulf. Excellent food, rather expensive, pay in hard currency.

Zhemchuzhina, 2 ShkiperskyProspekt,tel. 355-2063. Azerbaijani cuisine.

Oreshek, 11 Liinaya 60. Offers desserts, drinks and snacks.

Pribaltiiskaya Hotel. Has a number of restaurants that usually require advance reservations. Try the top floor bar (in the back) that serves quick hot food of chicken and meat dishes. Must pay in foreign currency.

Fontanka Canal
Fontanka, Fontanka 77, tel. 310-0689. Very popular co-operative restaurant that offers delicious food and floor shows nightly. Expensive. Reservations recommended.

Griboyedov Canal
Chaika, 14 Griboyedov Embankment. The "Seagull" Café.

Kolomna, 162 Griboyedov Emb. Pastries and herbal teas.

Other Co-operatives
Viktoria, 190 Moskovsky Prospekt. Pies and pastries

Vodi Lagidze, 3 Belinsky Street, tel. 279-1104. Serves excellent spicy food and flavored waters. (Water said to be imported from Germany and safe to drink.)

Imereti, 104 Prospekt Marxa. tel. 245-5003. Georgian cuisine.

Klassik, 202 Ligovsky Prospekt. tel. 166-0159. Open 11am-9 pm and closed 3-4.30pm. Serves a varied selection of hot meals.

Ogonek, 11 B. Zelyonniya Street, tel. 513-2921. Open 11am-11pm. Dessert spot with coffee, tea and juices.

Progress, 23 Prosvesheniya Prospekt, tel. 597-7210. Open 9 am-midnight. A variety of dishes, and baked and fruit desserts.

Polecye, 4 Sredneokhnsky Prospekt, tel. 224-2917. Open 12.30-10 pm. Specializes in White Russian dishes with musical videos on TV.

Pishechnaya, 19 Razyezzhaya Street, tel. 186-3427. A donut shop.

Salkhino, 8 Sovetsky Street. 27/29. Georgian cuisine.

Staraya Derevnya, 72 Sabushkina Street. "Old Village" Restaurant has literary and art gatherings.

Tbilisi, 10 Sitninskaya Square, tel. 232-9391. Open 11am-11pm. Very popular restaurant serving Georgian food.

Khachapuri, 6 Krasnoarmeisky Street. 13/18. tel. 292-7377. Open 12-11pm. Another popular Georgian restaurant.

Shopping

Beriozka Shops
Hotel Pribaltiiskaya (one is inside the hotel, two other large ones are outside on either side); Hotel Leningrad; Hotel Evropeiskaya; Hotel Moskva; also at 9 Nevsky Prospekt and 26 Herzen Street.

Main Department Stores
Gostiny Dvor 35 Nevsky Prospekt; **Passazh** 48 Nevsky Prospekt; **Dom Leningradskoi Torgovli** 21-23 Zhelyabov St; **Frunzensky Univermag** 60 Moskovsky Prospekt; **Moskovsky Univermag** 205-220 Moskovsky Prospekt; **Kirovsky Univermag** 9 Stachek Sq; **Narvsky Univermag** 12-34 Geroyev (Hero) Prospekt; **Sintetika** 4 Novoizmailovsky Prospekt.

Along Nevsky Prospekt
No. 8 and 45: paintings and applied art.
No. 9: Beriozka

No. 13: **Mir** books published by other socialist countries.

No. 24: Galstuki tie shop and ice-cream café.

No. 26: souvenir shop. Outside the Literary Café, on the corner of Nevsky and the Moika Canal, are artists that can paint your portrait.

No: 28: **Dom Knigi**. The House of Books is the largest bookstore in Leningrad, with books, foreign language publications, posters and postcards. It used to be the Singer Sewing Company. Notice the globe on the roof.

No. 30: fabric store.

No. 34: record store; next door is the Culinary Café.

Down to the left, on Brodsky Street, is the Evropeisky Hotel with a Beriozka, and café to get a quick bite to eat.

No. 35: **Gostiny Dvor**. The two-story yellow complex is the largest shopping arcade in the city. The Merchant's Yard dates from 1785. Facing the store to its left, along the side street, are a number of Commissioni second-hand stores.

No. 44: **Sever**. The best cake shop in town.

No. 48: **Passazh** department store for women.

No. 50: shop with books and postcards.

No. 52: crystal and ceramic shop.

No. 54: **Podarki** gift-shop.

No. 56: **Gastronom No. 1**. One of the oldest foodstores in Leningrad, formerly known as Yeliseyev's. It still has a lavish decor. Even though the food is lacking, it is well worth a peek.

Across the street, in Ostrovsky Square with the Statue of Catherine the Great, are many artist stalls, selling paintings, portraits and local crafts.

No. 58: **Molochni** ice-cream café.

No. 60: sporting-goods store; next to it is a movie theater.

No. 62-64: crystal, china, embroidery, tobacco and cigarettes—*papirosi* are the ones with the long cardboard filter.

No. 66-72: breadstore, sweets, clothing store, albums, prints, reproductions and postcards.

No. 78: bookstore.

No. 92: photography goods.

No. 96: paints and varnish.

No. 114: travel wares.

No. 147: crystal.

On the Death of Lenin

Comrades, we Communists are people of a special mould. We are made of a special stuff. We are those who form the army of the great proletarian strategist, the army of Comrade Lenin. There is nothing higher than the honour of belonging to this army. There is nothing higher than the title of member of the Party whose founder and leader was Comrade Lenin. It is not given to everyone to be a member of such a party. It is not given to everyone to withstand the stresses and storms that accompany membership in such a party. It is the sons of the working class, the sons of want and struggle, the sons of incredible privation and heroic effort who before all should be members of such a party. That is why the party of the Leninists, the party of the Communists, is also called the party of the working class.

DEPARTING FROM US, COMRADE LENIN ADJURED US TO HOLD HIGH AND GUARD THE PURITY OF THE GREAT TITLE OF MEMBER OF THE PARTY. WE VOW TO YOU, COMRADE LENIN, THAT WE WILL FULFIL YOUR BEHEST WITH CREDIT!

For twenty-five years Comrade Lenin moulded our Party and finally trained it to be the strongest and most highly steeled workers' party in the world. The blows of tsardom and its henchmen, the fury of the bourgeoisie and the landlords, the armed attacks of Kolchak and Denikin, the armed intervention of England and France, the lies and slanders of the hundred-mouthed bourgeois press—all those scorpions constantly chastised our Party for a quarter of a century. But our Party stood firm as a rock, repelling the countless blows of the enemy and leading the working class forward, to victory. In fierce battles our Party forged the unity and solidarity of its ranks. And by unity and solidarity it achieved the victory over the enemies of the working class.

DEPARTING FROM US, COMRADE LENIN ADJURED US TO GUARD THE UNITY OF OUR PARTY AS THE APPLE OF OUR EYE. WE VOW TO YOU, COMRADE LENIN, THAT THIS BEHEST, TOO, WE WILL FULFIL WITH CREDIT!

Joseph Stalin addressing the Second All-Union Congress of Soviets, January 26, 1924

Farmers' Market

A farmers' *riinok* (market) selling vegetables, fruit and flowers is at Kuznechny Lane, just behind Vladimirksky Metro stop, off Vladimirsky Prospekt.

Theaters and Concert Halls

Evening performances in theaters usually begin at 7.30, and concerts at 8.00 pm. The time of the performance and seat number are written on the ticket. You are usually required to check your coat in the cloakroom before entering the performance. Here you can also rent opera glasses for a small charge.

Bolshoi Puppet Theater, 10 Nekrasov Street
Children's Theater, 1 Pionersky Square
Circus, 3 River Fontanka Embankment
Comedy Theater, 56 Nevsky Prospekt
Glinka Academic Capella, 20 River Moika Embankment
Gorky Academic Bolshoi Drama Theater, 65 River Fontanka Embankment
Kirov Theater, 1 Teatralnaya (Theater) Square
Komissarzhevskaya Drama Theater, 19 Rakov Street
Komsomol Theater, 4 Lenin Park
Lensoviet Theater, 12 Vladimirsky Prospekt
Maly Theater for Opera and Ballet, 1 Iskusstv (Arts) Square
Oktyabrsky Concert Hall, 6 Ligovsky Prospekt
Puppet Theater, 52 Nevsky Prospekt
Pushkin Drama Theater, 2 Ostrovsky Square
Rimsky-Korsakov Conservatory, 3 Teatralnaya (Theater) Square
Shostakovich Philharmonia, 2 Brodsky Street
Glinka Maly Philharmonia 30 Nevsky Prospekt
Theater of Musical Comedy, 13 Rakov Street
Variety Theater, 27 Zhelyabov Street

Sports

Chigorin Chess Club, 25 Zhelyabov Street.
Dynamo Stadium, Park Pobedy (Victory Park)
Kirov Stadium, 13 Morskoi Prospekt on Krestovsky Island
Lenin Sports and Concert Complex, 8 Gagarin Prospekt on Pet
    rovsky Island
Palace of Culture, 42 Kirov Avenue on Vasilyevsky Island
Yubileiny Sports Palace, 18 Dobrolyubov Prospekt
Winter Stadium, 11 Inzhenernaya Street.

    Also check at the Intourist desk for indoor and outdoor pool, and *banya* (sauna/pool) locations. One *banya* complex is on Marat Street just off Nevsky Prospekt (no. 100) and Metro stop Mayakovskaya. It is open 7 am–11 pm, closed on Mondays and Tuesdays. Each part has two saunas and a small swimming pool.

Recommended Reading

General History and Current Affairs

Billington, James. *The Icon and the Axe: An interpretive History of Russian Culture,* Vintage, 1966.

Binyon, Michael. *Life in Russia,* Random House, 1983.

Brown, Edward. *Russian Literature Since the Revolution,* Macmillan 1969.

Cohen, Stephen. *Sovieticus: American Perceptions and Soviet Realities,* W.W. Norton, 1986.

de Jonge, Alex. *The Life and Times of Grigorii Rasputin,* Dorset Press 1987.

Goldman, Marshall. *Gorbachev's Challenge: Economic Reform in the Age of High Technology,* W.W. Norton, 1987.

Gorbachev, Mikhail. *Perestroika: New Thinking for Our Country and the World,* Harper and Row, 1987.

Hammer, Armand and Neil Lyndon. *Hammer*, Putnam, 1987.

Hayward, Max. *Writers in Russia: 1917-1978*, Harvest, 1984.

Kaiser. *The People and the Power,* Pocket, 1976.

Lenin. *What Is To Be Done?* Written 1902, published by Pengiun, 1988.

Lincoln, W. Bruce. *The Romanovs,* Dial Press, 1981.

Massie, Robert. *Nicholas and Alexandra,* Atheneum, 1967.

Massie, Robert. *Peter the Great,* Ballantine, 1980.

Massie, Suzanne. *Land of the Firebird: The Beauty of Old Russia,* Simon and Shuster, 1980.

Massie, Suzanne. *The Living Mirror: Five Young Poets from Leningrad,* Doubleday, 1972

Medvedev, Roy. *Let People Judge*, Alfred Knopf, 1971.

Medvedev, Z & R. *A Question of Madness*, W.W. Norton, 1979.

Mirsky, D.S. *A History of Russian Literature*, Alfred Knopf, 1958.

Reed, John. *The Ten Days That Shook the World*. Written 1919, published by International, 1967.

Riasanovsky, N. *A History of Russia*, Oxford University Press, 1984.

Richard & Vaillant. *From Russia to the USSR*, Independent School Press, 1987.

Riehn, Richard. *1812: Napoleon's Russian Campaign*. McGraw Hill, 1990.

Salisbury, Harrison. *Nine Hundred Days: The Siege of Leningrad*, Avon, 1970.

Ulam, Adam. *The Bolsheviks*, Macmillan, 1965.

Walker, Martin. *The Waking Giant*, Sphere, 1987.

Yeltsin, Boris. *Against the Grain*, Summit Books, 1990.

Picture Books; Art and Culture

A Day in the Life of the Soviet Union, Collins, 1987.

Saved for Humanity: The Hermitage During the Siege of Leningrad 1941-1944, Aurora, Leningrad, 1985.

A Portrait of Tsarist Russia, Pantheon, 1989.

Stanislavsky on the Art of the Stage, translated by D. Margarshack, Hill & Wang, 1961.

Harlow Robinson's *Sergei Prokofiev: A Biography*, Paragon, 1988.

Russian Masters: Glinka, Borodin, Balakirev, Mussorgsky, Tchaikovsky, W.W. Norton, 1986.

Russian Fairy Tales, Pantheon, 1973.

Citizen Diplomats: Pathfinders in Soviet American Relations - And How You Can Join Them, Continuum, 1987.

Bird, Alan. *A History of
Russian Painting,* Oxford,
London, 1987.

Chamberlain, Leslie. *The
Food and Cooking of
Russia,* Penguin, London,
1983.

Gray, Camilla. *The
Russian Experiment in Art
1863-1922,* Thames and
Hudson, 1986.

Popova, Olga. *Russian
Illuminated Manuscripts,*
Thames and Hudson,
1984.

Skvorecky, Josef. *Talking
Moscow Blues,* Ecco
Press, 1988.

Snowman, A. Kenneth.
*Carl Fabergé: Goldsmith
to the Imperial Court of
Russia,* Crown, 1983.

Troitsky, Artemus. *Back in the USSR: The True Story of Rock in Russia,* Faber
& Faber, 1987.

Novels and Travel Writing

The Portable Chekhov, Viking, Penguin, 1968.

The Portable Tolstoy, and *War and Peace,* Penguin, 1978.

Anna Akhmatova: Poems, translated by Lyn Coffin, Introduction by Joseph
    Brodsky, W.W. Norton, 1983.

Dostoevsky, Fyodor. *Crime and Punishment,* Translated by C. Garnett,
    Bantam, 1982.

Filippov, Boris. *Leningrad in Literature. The Complete Prose Tales of Alexandr Sergeyevitch Pushkin,* translated by G. Aitken, W.W. Norton, 1966.

Gogol, Nikolai. *Dead Souls,* translated by D. Magarshack, Penguin, 1961.

Hansson and Liden. *Moscow Women,* Random House, 1983.

Kelly, Laurence. *Moscow: A Traveller's Companion,* Constable & Co, London, 1983, and *St Petersburg: A Traveller's Companion,* Atheneum, N.Y., 1983.

Mochulsky, K. *Dostoevsky: His Life and Work,* Princeton University Press, 1967.

Pasternak, Boris. *Dr Zhivago,* translated by M. Hayward, Ballantine, 1988.

Rybakov, Anatoly. *Children of the Arbat,* Dell, 1988.

Salisbury, Harrison. *Moscow Journal,* University of Chicago Press, 1961.

Solzhenitsyn, Alexander. *One Day in the Life of Ivan Denisovich,* Bantam, 1963, *The First Circle,* Harper & Row, 1968, and *The Gulag Archipelago,* Harper and Row, 1973.

"The Bronze Horseman"

Where lonely waters, struggling, sought
To reach the sea, he (Peter the Great) paused, in thought...
The haughty Swede here we'll curb and hold at bay
And here, to gall him, found a city.
As nature bids so must we do:
A window will we cut here through
On Europe, and a foothold gaining
Upon this coast, the ships we'll hail
Of every flag, and freely sail
These seas, no more ourselves restraining.
A century passed, and there it stood,
Of Northern lands the pride and beauty,
A young, resplendent, gracious city,
Sprung out the dark of mire and wood...
Now there rise great palaces and towers; a maze
Of sails and mastheads crown the harbor;
Ships of all ports moor here beside
These rich and peopled shores; the wide,
Majestic Neva slowly labors,
In granite clad, to push its way
'Neath graceful bridges; gardens cover
The once bare isles that dot the river,
Its glassy surface still and grey.
Old Moscow fades beside her rival.
A dowager, she is outshone,
Overshadowed by the new arrival
Who, robed in purple, mounts the throne...

Alexander Pushkin (1833)

Taubman, W & J. *Moscow Spring*,
Summit, 1989.

Thubron, Colin. *Where Nights are
Longest,* Atlantic Monthly Press, 1983.

Turgenev, Ivan. *Fathers and Sons*,
translated by D. Magarshack, Penguin,
1961.

Ustinov, Peter. *My Russia*, Little Brown
& Co, 1983.

Van Der Post, Laurens. *Journey in
Russia*, Penguin, 1965.

Voinovich, Vladimir. *Moscow 2042*,
Harcourt Brace Jovanovich, 1987.

Wechsberg, Joseph. *In Leningrad*,
Doubleday, 1977.

Wilson, A.N. *Tolstoy Biography,*
Ballantine, 1988.

Films and Videos Available for Rental or Purchase

National Geographic's *Inside the Soviet Circus,* 1988, and *Voices of Leningrad,* 1990

Durrell in Russia

Moscow: The Other Russians

Reds 1981

Moscow on the Hudson, 1984.

Basic Russian by Video.

Eisenstein's *Potemkin,* USSR, 1925.

October: Ten Days that Shook the World, USSR, 1927.

Alexander Nevsky, USSR, 1938.

Ivan the Terrible, USSR, 1946.

Eisenstein, USSR, 1958.

Pudovkin's *Mother,* USSR, 1926.

The End of St Petersburg, USSR, 1927.

Vertov's *The Man with the Movie Camera,* USSR, 1928.

Petrov's *Peter the First: Parts I, II,* USSR, 1937.

Tarkovsky's *Andrei Rublev,* USSR, 1965.

Maya Plisetskaya Dances, USSR.

Backstage at the Kirov, USSR, 1984.

Menshov's *Moscow Doesn't Believe in Tears,* 1980.

Abuladze's *Repentance,* USSR, 1987.

Pichul's *Little Vera,* USSR, 1988.

20th Century Fox, *Icons,* 1991, shot in Moscow.

Index

60p

SOLD BY
SURREY COUNTY LIBRARY
WITH ALL FAULTS